REVIEW

SAILING

Earning the Golden Sail: It is the goal of many of us--retiring from the rat race, buying a sailboat, and sailing off into the sunset. But the questions loom large. What type of boat? Where do we sail? How will we manage?

These are all questions sailing contributor, Matts Djos and his wife Jeanine, faced when he retired in 2006 and his search for answers is recorded in his new book, "Sailing Out of Retirement."

Starting with a trailerable Balboa 26, Matts and Jeanine move up to a Mariner 31 ketch, which they restore and fit out for cruising. Some of the chapters have appeared previously in SAILING Magazine and may be familiar to readers, but they've been updated for the book. For retirees and the curious of all ages, the book will serve as a guide and case study of one couple's endeavor to live the dream (May 2011).

CRUISING WORLD:

In a nation of baby boomers, this volume targets an often ignored niche: senior sailors. The crux of the book is a primer based on the septuagenarian author's experiences gleaned when, after retirement, he and his wife bought a Mariner 31 ketch and went cruising. Djos advises on choosing and buying a pre-owned boat, refitting, selecting a marina, heavy weather tactics, and medical issues for older cruisers.

SOUNDINGS MAGAZINE:

Seasoned sailors with the wind still in their sails might consider "Sailing Out of Retirement: Living the Dream" by the veteran cruising couple, Matts and Jeanine Djos. The two have extensively sailed the West Coast from Canada to Mexico, and Matts has written extensively as a freelance writer for multiple nautical magazines. In their new book, the retired couple offers suggestions on how to find the right used boat--drawing from their own experience--from an extensive restoration to a shakedown cruise.

Also chronicled are the nuances of marinas and moorings; short and long term cruising, common sense seamanship, matters of personal health, safety and onboard ambiance and comfort--all geared toward retirees and seniors.

The Djoses currently sail a trailerable 26 foot Balboa and a Mariner 31, which is moored in San Pedro, Calif.

48 NORTH, THE SAILING MAGAZINE:

Sailing Out of Retirement" will be of special interest to novices, adventurers, retirees, armchair sailors, and lovers of the wind and sea. Given their experience over fifty years under sail, Matts and Jeanine Djos describe how to find just the right pre-owned boat, including what may be involved in an extensive refit, restoration, and shakedown . . .

Sailing Out of Retirement
Living the Dream

For my wife and editor, Jeanine, who has been my soul mate and shipmate these many precious years; I would also like to dedicate this book to our children, Monika, Joanna, and Heidi, remarkable women, all!

Sailing Out of Retirement
Living the Dream

Matts G. Djos
with Jeanine J. Djos

Revised 2012
Photos by Matts & Jeanine Djos

Copyright Matts G. Djos, 2010
All rights reserved

Acknowledgements

I would like to thank the editors of <u>Sailing</u> magazine, <u>Cruising World</u>, <u>Sail</u>, and <u>48 North</u> for their editorial encouragement and permission to reprint some of the material presented here. I would also like to thank Tom Orrell of Colorado Mesa University for his assistance and advice in helping me to format this book. Finally, I would like to thank my wife, Jeanine, for her photographic assistance and for her unerring judgment in helping me to refine and edit the final drafts of this book.

md

Table of Contents

A Note on the Djoses . . . . iv-v
Preface 1-3
Introduction 4-8
Chapter I-- Prelude: The Thinking
    Sailor: Surviving the Odds 9-24
Chapter II-- Buying the Right Boat:
    Stepping Up to a Safer, more
    Comfortable Rig 25-44
Chapter III--The Refit 45-56
Chapter IV--Finding the Right Moorage . .57-70
Chapter V-- First Aid and Safety 71-92
Chapter VI-- The Shakedown:
    Homeward Bound 93-107
Chapter VII-- Sailing at 70 108-117

- - - - - - - - - - - - -

Appendix I: A Note for Novices 118-127
Appendix II: Heavy Weather Tactics . . . 128-133
Appendix III: Choosing Just the
    Right Sailboat 134-163
Appendix IV: Calculating Boat
    and Sail Performance 164-169
Appendix V: *Scandia Dream's*
    Checklist 170-171
Appendix VI: Suggested Reading. 172-177
Index 178-180

A Note on the Djoses:

Matts G. and Jeanine J. Djos are lifelong sailors and boating enthusiasts. The two have sailed throughout much of the West, including Mexico, southern California, the Pacific Northwest, Canada, the desert Southwest, and the Rocky Mountain High Country.

Matts has free-lanced for a variety of major national publications, including Sail, Cruising World, Sailing magazine, and 48 North. He has written five other books, including Writing Under the Influence, (Palgrave/Macmillan, 2010), Fixing Positions: Trailer Sailing the West (Sheridan House, 2008), The Sacrament of Sail: Finding Our Way (Amazon, 2011), the revised version of the "Sacrament" book, Cruising the West: Fifty Years of Sail (Amazon, 2011), and the contemporary novel, The Spindrift (2012).

Matts, has been in public education for more than forty-five years, the last thirty as a professor of English, Emeritus, at Colorado Mesa University in Grand Junction.

When they aren't sailing, the Djoses live in the Colorado Rockies southeast of Grand Junction.

Preface

The chapters to follow are especially for retirees and seniors who love to sail or would like to sail. They are also something of an adventure story. Some of the material was published in national sailing magazines, but it has all been updated and revised according to the observations that Jeanine and I have made in the intervening years. Following the Introduction and our reasons for writing this book, we will begin with a storm that took the measure of us, for it has a good deal to do with the kind of luck and tenacity that most of us seniors know all too well. It also forced us to rethink our cruising plans and the necessity of 'stepping up' to a larger boat when we celebrated my retirement in 2006.

The remaining chapters invite the reader to share our experiences and insights as we buy, refit, and relocate our 'new' boat, especially as those observations relate to matters of extended cruising, health and safety, our love of the sea, and good seamanship. Some of the chapters will contain a sidebar or two, and the appendix will offer technical advice on storm management and some additional material on boat buying for seniors, a brief sailing lesson for novices with suggestions on the basics of sailing, methods for calculating boat and sail performance, *Scandia Dream's* checklist for getting under way and returning, and a suggested reading list.

I have dealt sparingly with the fundamentals of navigation, and sail management. Those who are new to sailing or who are only somewhat familiar with the basics will find innumerable instructional manuals at their local library or bookstore. However, I would strongly recommend John Rusmaniere's <u>The Annapolis Book of Seamanship</u> for starters. It is one of the best. They may also want to check my list of suggested readings at the end of this book.

As for Jeanine and me, our story, of course, isn't ended. Life, fortunately, isn't that way. No matter how vibrant our former years under sail, Jeanine and I are certain that the years to follow will be just as fascinating as the years past. I suppose we will have time enough to reminisce in a decade or two; but, for now, the two of us are content to celebrate the gift of each new day, the wonder of a freshening breeze, and the infinite pleasure of an emerald sea on a sunny afternoon.

Introduction

And thou thy soul sail leagues and leagues beyond--
Still, leagues beyond those leagues, there is more sea.

Dante Gabriel Rossetti

We live in a twenty-first century fiefdom of electronic servitude that has unwittingly shackled us to such a chaos of speed and efficiency that we scarce know who we are or where we are going. Such is the grim, good fortune of civilized living; but, lest we forget, there is always the profound detachment and freedom of sail where we can escape the fissures of our civilized routine, celebrate the wind, and adopt the perspective of the prophet and sage. Our instincts tell us that it is in such hours that we are best able to examine the depth of our gypsy soul–albeit in the privacy of the cosmos. If we are successful in our digging and if we can work past the alluvium of our daily affairs, we shall discover an expanse so grand we may not even recognize our own perception. Given just the right time and place, we might even regress to our natural state and embrace with exquisite detachment a moment of grace, for while it is not often experienced, it will be well worth the seeking–if only for its incalculable depth.

Richard Henry Dana wrote that there is witchery in the sea; and it may well be that such is the essence of our life work in progress--that, in hoisting sail, Jeanine and I are in the closest possible relation with each other, even as we are entangled in a moment of exquisite beauty.
Perhaps, in such an instant, we are able to enjoy a momentary stay from the chafing intrusions of time and responsibility; and we can stand on an equal footing with all of life, both great and small. It may then be possible to discover a new and more expansive relation to the wind, that we might disclose the full magnitude of a distant horizon,

find comfort in a protected anchorage with only the night hawks to keep us company, and marvel at the clarity of our intimate relation with the cosmos as it dances merrily overhead.

Let us never forget that the wind and the sea will have us out in the ephemeral wonder of each morning and the gentle cadence of the waves until all our fears and worries ebb away with the evening tide, and we are lost in the steady quietude of an ocean reverie. Perhaps in landlessness alone lies the highest truth; but, if the wind howls and the sea leaps, we must be content to mind the helm and dismiss all deep thinking, lest our spirit ebb away to that deep, blue bottomless soul from whence it came. In such bewildering moments, we may be compelled to leave that miser-man, *Wisdom*, in our wake; and be about the earnest
business of navigation, for we will be lucky enough to understand where we are, let alone where we *shall be*.

In the meantime, let us hoist sail, peer owl-like into the distant horizon, and drive before the wind as if we were prepared to mount direct to heaven. Let us snuff at the air as the bubbling foam splashes from our bows in a watery cascade. Noah's flood has not yet subsided; two-thirds of the world yet it covers, so let us be about the business of discovering the azure depths beneath our keel, the untempered watery world, and the heartless immensity of the horizon. Drink deep, then, dear reader, for as seasoned sailors, we must be perpetually about the earnest business of navigation and the sublime pleasure of a perfect day and a bracing wind.

Chapter I

The Thinking Sailor: Surviving the Odds

There lies the port; the vessel puffs her sail...
  Old age hath yet his honor and his toil....
We are not now that strength which in old days
  Moved earth and heaven, that which we are, we are;...Made weak by time and fate, but strong in will to strive, to seek, to find, and not to yield.
    from "Ulysses," Alfred Lord Tennyson, 1833

Jeanine and I had been exploring the Middle Gulf of the Sea of Cortez aboard our trailerable Balboa 26 and were sailing north from Bahia Concepcion when we learned that a massive Pacific low was barreling east and was expected to strike the Baja coast in thirty-six hours. A couple of blue water rigs out of Punta Chivato planned to weigh anchor and clear for the mainland shortly before sunset, and a commercial fishery told us that he planned to do much the same. Jeanine and I discussed whether we should follow them or trust our instincts and wait out the storm in a nearby safe-hole. Still, San Carlos, which lay abut ninety miles northeast of us, gave us about a twenty hour window of safety; and we wouldn't be that far from our three companions. Besides, our chances for a safe passage looked pretty good--providing we cleared the reef at Santa Inez before dark.

We decided to follow the three larger boats, convinced ourselves that everything would be ok, and headed for open water, bound (optimistically) for San Carlos some twelve to fourteen hours across the gulf. At first, everything went as expected. By 7:00 pm, the offshore breeze had played out; and we had dropped our sails and were motoring toward Tortuga Island when a rather strange 5-7 knot breeze began to pipe out of the west. By 9:00, it had increased 10-15; and, a half hour later, it was piping 15 to 20.

Jeanine had been listening to the VHF for some time, and she overheard a conversation between two of the other boats who were about a mile ahead of us. It seems that they felt "rather sorry for that small boat. They are really in for it." It was obvious that they were talking about us!

We hailed them and learned that their weather fax had forecast a second low pressure system off the coast of southern California; and, because of a ridge of high pressure in the Four Corners, the two systems had merged, were racing southeast, and were expected to strike the central gulf sometime before midnight.

A short while later, we made contact with a ketch named *Harmony*, who had picked up a second weather report from the north. She reported that the isobars to the west of us were much tighter than originally predicted, and we could expect at least Force 8 winds (34-40 knots) sometime after midnight. We were already taking quite a pounding, and I could only discern her stern light when we topped some of the larger swells.

Other than that, we were now entirely alone.

Jeanine and I discussed whether we should turn back, bash wind and wave for some 15 to 20 miles, and try to negotiate Tortuga Island and the reef at Santa Inez in the dark. Neither option had much appeal, but we decided that it would be better to continue east--especially since the wind and waves were out of the northwest. I stowed all anchors below and tied two painters to the inflatable in the event that one of them failed. I also elected to drag it on a short line rather than pull it aboard and secure it over the bow hatch. This would have been the preferred alternative on a larger boat; but, on a 26 foot trailerable, it would be extremely difficult to launch if we foundered.

I reeled in the headsail and double reefed the main to minimize splash-over and maximize control, since this would heel the boat very slightly, move the center of effort forward, and reduce transom motor pressure. I also entered the Cabo Haro and Guaymas coordinates on the GPS in the unlikely event that our engine failed, and we had to turn south away from Bahia San Carlos and run for the mainland and Guaymas Harbor under sail alone.

By 10:30, the wind was piping 40 to 45 knots difference between the troughs and the cresting, breaking waves at 10-13 feet. Most of them made a loud rushing and boiling sound as they slammed in from the northwest and broke against our port beam and transom, sometimes lifting us high enough to cavitate the propeller. At such times, I had to pull back on the throttle, wait for an instant, and reset it, while the Balboa turned with the wind and lurched broadside to the waves.

An hour later, the seas were running 12 to 15 feet, and it had gotten very cold. I was thoroughly soaked from the breaking waves, which crashed into the cockpit with increasing regularity. Jeanine tossed me a dry parka and a couple of extra sweaters (I had trouble enough without having to deal with hypothermia) and closed the hatches to minimize the cold and avoid splash-over from the larger waves. I put on the parka and the sweaters, snapped back into my safety harness, wedged my back on the port coaming, and locked my knees against the starboard bench to keep from getting thrown overboard as some of the larger waves plunged beneath our keel.

In the meantime, it was pandemonium below deck: books, dishes, cushions, canned goods, blankets, and cookware were tossed helter-skelter—even the porta-potti was thrown against the starboard wardrobe; but Jeanine secured what little was possible, stuffed the keel cable well opening with towels to minimize spillover, and loosened the cable ever so slightly to minimize vibration and rumble as we surfed down the backside of the rollers. She also managed to double-checked both thru-hulls to make sure that they were closed and tight; set out extra PFD's, a first-aid kit, emergency plugs and flares, filled a gallon jug with extra water, and stuffed a watertight ditch bag with our passports and vital personal belongings.

We had been burning a gallon of gas about every fifty minutes; and I had managed to crawl forward, open the hatch, and switch from the main tank to the smaller utility earlier that night; but I knew that I would have to refill both of them about every four hours. This was especially important since we did not want to risk draining the fuel line and killing the engine (I'd already refueled the main tank earlier that evening as we passed

Tortuga Island, but that was in relatively benign conditions).

I calculated that we would have to fill the utility tanks shortly after midnight and once again at about 4:30 am. These would be risky propositions, since I would have to put the engine in neutral, unbuckle my safety harness, crawl to the starboard hatch, and open it while Jeanine removed the hatch boards and held the flashlight as she clung to one of the handholds at the entry hatch. I would then have to lug the tanks to the cockpit sole, unseal the jerry cans, refill the utilities (spilling as little as possible), seal both tanks, replace the jerry cans, and reclaim the helm--all while the boat lurched to starboard and heeled broadside to the waves.

The first refill started without much of a hitch. After throttling back to about two knots, I managed to top both tanks and spilled only about a pint of gas in the process. I rinsed my shoes and the cockpit sole, and Jeanine doused the flashlight and reset the hatch boards. I reclaimed the helm, snapped back into my harness, and pushed the throttle forward. It didn't respond. I checked the throttle cable and discovered that the plastic casing had split. I called to Jeanine, and she grabbed some tape from the emergency drawer below and tossed it to me. I triple wrapped the casing, tossed back the tape, pushed the throttle slowly forward; and, thankfully, it responded without breaking through the tape.

The Sea of Cortez is known to generate "square" waves with narrow troughs and a tendency to break prematurely. Still, as the night wore on, I gradually developed a technique for dealing with the surge by climbing each wave at an angle to avoid being pooped as it overtook us and then turning to starboard and surfing at an angle down the opposing or backside so we wouldn't pitch pole as it passed to the east. I did this time and time again, spinning the wheel port and starboard with each cresting wave to work them past us one at a time. I did not allow myself to think of the next wave or how many more I would have to deal with before the night was over, nor did I think about the mainland and the prospect of doing this over and over for some 50 or 60 miles. I simply dealt with each of them one-by-one and concentrated on controlling the helm, lest we breach and be lost.

Because of the lurching and bouncing, the GPS could not maintain a fix for more than a minute or two; and I was forced to reset it again and again. The magnetic compass was practically useless because of the constant bouncing and heeling; and I finally, I gave up, targeted a series of stars directly over the horizon northeast of us, and tossed the GPS to Jeanine rather than risk losing it overboard. While I could not be sure of our exact location at any one time, I continued to calculate our progress by dead reckoning and by keeping the boat at a constant angle to the waves as they broke off our port quarter.

I knew that fear was our worst enemy, since I might over-react and broach or lose my focus and lose control of the boat. I also knew that most people give up long before their boat, although I would have to use every bit of skill I had--and hope for a bit of luck--to get us safely home. With a less stable boat and perhaps a narrower perspective of years, we might not have survived. In fact, I was later to discover that two other, larger boats farther south had to be airlifted out. I refueled the utility tanks a second time just before dawn and spilled about a quart of gas on the cabin sole because of the horrible rocking and pitching. As I gently reset the throttle--taking care not to break the tape casing, I looked up and saw a brief, dim flash from the lighthouse at Punta Haro on the mainland some twenty miles south. I knew then that we were going to make it home.

Shortly after dawn, in the first, dim light of day, I looked astern for an instant and saw the full height and fury of the cresting waves as they broke against the hull. They were awful. In fact, it was probably best that I was blissfully unaware of their full power until we were almost home. As it was, we battled the next 15 or so miles as before, but with a good deal more optimism.

Lumpy seas, a terrifically cold morning, and a windless sea at early dawn the week before. Matts at the helm of our Balboa 26, *Lady Jeanine*, about twenty miles out from Santa Rosalia, the Baja Peninsula, and Bajia Concepcion.

As we covered the last mile and rounded the lee of Punta Doble just west of San Carlos and headed for our slip at Marina Seca, my grip on the wheel loosened, and I took my feet off the starboard bench while Jeanine poured me a cup of coffee.

I couldn't help but feel that we had managed--perhaps with a few blessings--to escape with our lives by the narrowest of margins; still, our little boat had seen us through, and, for that, I was grateful.

After the boat was secured at the dock, it was just about impossible to settle down or get any rest, even though we had been awake for more than 36 hours. We put the boat in order, showered, had breakfast at the hotel, and drove up to the scenic overlook at Punta Doble west of San Carlos to take a second look at the gulf. It was awash with flume and white stallions as far as I could see; the wind howled out of the northwest at about 45 to 50 knots; and I was astonished that anyone in a small boat--certainly not us--could possibly survive such conditions. Jeanine turned away, but I was transfixed. Something more than skill, more than our boat, more than five decades of experience, had seen us through--of this I was certain. And, yet, I was grateful that I knew enough about boat handling and had enough maturity to put my feelings aside with a measure of tenacity and skill. Very likely, had this happened even ten years earlier, we might well have made a critical misstep and perhaps perished.

As it was, we arrived safely to see another day-

-shaken and a bit wiser, but safe and, surprisingly, undamaged. It was not until a number of months later, however, that I grasped the full significance of that terrible night and how we had been put to the test. Only then did I begin to have sleep problems--delayed stress, I believe, as I relived the entire ordeal in excruciating detail and allowed myself to feel the near hopelessness of our situation.

Later, as we discussed the events of that crossing, Jeanine and I concluded that, given unreliable weather reports, the decisions of other boaters, or second hand information, a thirty-six hour window was not sufficient to assure a safe 90 or 100 mile crossing—the next time, I will insist on a much larger window of safety or stay put.

I have talked with enough veteran sailors to realize that most have been pushed far beyond the customary limits of endurance and are all too familiar with the unforgiving power of the sea. While they still nurture a renegade spirit, they also know their limits and readily acknowledge their frailty. They also recognize that no matter how crusty or old, how professional or circumspect, they will never be fully knowledgeable about the infinite nuances of the wind and the sea, their personal limits, and the limits of their boat.

As for Jeanine and me, we try to make our sailing decisions according to the best information available at the time, although it can be remarkably limited and untrustworthy. We certainly do not head out on impulse or test our survival skills in some kind of bone-headed confrontation with the sea.

Sailing is demanding; and the sea is no place for fools, novices, or madmen. Those of us who love the sea understand the risks as well as the rewards in hoisting canvas and setting out for a distant horizon. Any sailing instructor will insist that the well-schooled skipper cannot not simply be skilled and knowledgeable. In some measure, that is the easy part. Good judgment, maturity, a healthy respect for the natural world, self-reliance, and a solid disdain for pointless risk-taking are of the essence. Xtreme sports have no place on the water; indeed, sailing involves a constant and very steep learning curve. We can always get better, because there is no limit to the complexities of the wind and the sea and the physics of a well-found boat.

There must ultimately come a time when our health or memory might eventually force us to stay ashore. I do suspect, however, that some of us quit the sea prematurely or wonder unnecessarily if they may be too old, when age is not yet relevant. I also wonder about those who quit their jobs, sell their homes, and head for the ocean to commence passage-making in a kind of mid-life move of desperation because they are convinced that, in a few years, they may be too old to manage a boat on their own. For most, this is a false assumption. The majority of enthusiasts can take to the water for a very long time yet to come. In fact, there is really no reason to quit the sea at the first sign of a slowdown.

The oldest among us are invariably the wisest and most skilled; and, while we may not possess the reflexes and strength of our youth, there are some wonderful compensations which can add immeasurably to the joy of sailing. Like the Ulysses of old, we certainly have the will, and we have the perspective, savvy, and experience—and detachment--to deal with any number of crises; for the sea has taken the measure of us all, tested our resources, our skills, our judgment; and--while not necessarily welcome--those tests are manifold and memorable in the extreme.

That terrible night on the Sea of Cortez took the measure of Jeanine and me. We learned a good deal more than we might want to learn about risk taking--it never did have much appeal; but we are both alive and well despite our close call. Still, I understand that sailing and exploring are part of our 50,000 year old inheritance--likely built into our genes, since the non-risk takers never left the safety of their caves, probably starved to death, and dropped out of the gene pool. Now, in the twenty-first century, however, we need to learn how to use that heritage to our benefit and make quick, effective decisions while celebrating life.

As any senior knows all too well, life's journey insists on moderation, which, if entered judiciously, is typically sufficient. We need not give up wind and water simply because we are overwhelmed by a larger rig that requires a crew of seven, the wisdom of Solomon, and the expertise of Captain Blye. Perhaps a smaller, simpler boat will suffice; a sturdy but slower rig, updated equipment and hydraulic assistance where raw muscle power was once sufficient. We might consider as well a shorter venue rather than a 48 hour endurance contest, a summer sail (only the Vikings appear to have relished a rollicking tour of the north Atlantic) when the winds hover at 10 knots and the waves barely crest. Such a festival of wonder might well be perfect for a smaller, well-found boat that is bound for a kindly week of cruising or an overnight destination in a cozy harbor.

Jeanine and I shall continue to sail for the sheer pleasure of it, the mental challenges, and our love of the wind and the sea. It is foolish to live desperately, but that does not mean that we should not live deliberately. Most of us find that it is just about impossible to plan more than ten years ahead. That is true for people in their twenties and thirties, and it is true for us now.

There are no second chances in this life; we are here but for an instant, and the bounty and wonderment of sailing are at our fingertips. Like the famed Ulysses of old, we are still strong in will, so let us drink life to the lees, for age hath yet his honor and his toil, and--for us--life piled on life were all too little. There lies the port, the vessel puffs her sail, and while much is taken, much still abides.

Chapter II

Buying the *Right* Boat: Stepping Up to a Safer, More Comfortable Rig

. . . she scatters the sprays
the chaff in the stroke of the flail;
Now white as the sea-gull, she flies on her way,
The sun gleaming bright on her sails.
"Sun and Shadow," Oliver Wendell Holmes

After that terrible night on the Sea of Cortez, Jeanine and I decided that if we were going to sail beyond our usual boundaries, we'd better find a safer, sturdier boat with a manageable sail plan, a solid pedigree, and good lines. While our trailerable was comfortable enough for short cruises, a little more size and few more amenities might also be nice--along with a blue water capability, durability, and ease of handling.

We started by surveying the market to get an idea of the kind of boat that best suited our requirements as senior sailors

This involved no small amount of persistence and something of a reality check as we tried to match our ideal with manageability, accommodations, and affordability. We learned that boat prices jump exponentially with every increase in length; and a 38 footer was likely to be a good deal more expensive than a 35, which was more expensive than a 32 footer, and so on. The same held true for age, although differences tended to be less significant once a boat reached 25 years or more.

We also learned to be careful about bargains. Boats that were underpriced for their size and age were suspect, and most 35-foot rigs that were priced like a 32 were not in very good condition.

We decided that it would be wiser to focus on a smaller if not older, well-found boat that we could afford; and, since anything more than twenty years old was going to be difficult to finance; we also expected to dig into our savings to close the sale. Once we had a reasonably good idea of what kind of boat best matched our budget and our ideal, we surveyed the Internet and focused on the specifics. *Yachtworld.com, Boats.com,* and *Usedboats.com* were especially helpful; although most of the boats listed did not entirely meet our personal requirements. Some were quite seaworthy, but rather too homely to have much appeal; some were far too high-tech for single-handed, senior sailing; and some were little more than floating RV's.

Note the tremendous difference between our final choice: the 1970, classic Mariner 31 ketch on the left and the sleek, late model Beneteau on the right.

We also realized that we were likely to find a more reliable performer if we chose a reputable production boat that was designed by a proven architect.

Most production models had an owner's web page that was loaded with information on the boat's strengths, necessary upgrades, common repairs, and the like. In fact, I was quite surprised at the amount of information offered by the Morgan, Ericson, Mariner, Hunter, and Catalina webs. We also found a good deal of information in the popular sailing magazines and bookstores.

In developing a short list of preferred boats, we found that the wording of the advertisements sometimes offered clues about the condition of a specific boat. For instance, we suspected that "Great live aboard" probably meant that the boat was just too tired to leave the dock; "Hawaii Veteran," "Mexico Veteran," "Alaska Veteran" and the like probably indicated that a boat had come a long way, been sailed hard, and was likely in need of a major refit. "Owner motivated" could mean that the boat was available at a negotiated price far below its market value, although it might also suggest that the boat was defective in some way and was difficult to sell.

As we completed our search, we began to wonder if certain boats that had been listed for a long time had something fundamentally wrong with them. I recall seeing an ad for a gorgeous Ericson 35 that had run for months, even though it seemed perfect in every way–at least from the descriptions and photographs. A friend eventually checked her out for me, and it turned out that she was delaminating around the stanchions and had far too many blisters to make her a worthwhile risk.

We also realized that we had some rather specific needs and concerns that were unique to our cruising style. Since Jeanine and I are retired seniors and not quite as quick or muscular as we were in our forties, we were very concerned about the sail plan, sail manageability, and ease of performance (this is one of the reasons that we eventually settled on a ketch). We also love comfort, so we took a close look at interior layouts, including the placement and amenities of the galley, the type of stove (safety was a major concern), the placement and seating around the salon table, lighting and ventilation, V-berth comfort, and the amount of storage space and ease of access. We were concerned about the head and the MSD (marine sanitation device), since our trailerable had only a porta-potty that was rather cumbersome and would hardly be sufficient for extended cruising. Finally, certain designs were more sea-kindly than others. A heavy boat, although slower, just about guaranteed a smoother ride; a shoal keel assured greater stability, although it could be the devil to back up and would not turn very quickly. A deep keel and shallow draft hull would likely pound in a heavy sea. Catamarans were invariably faster and more comfortable than monohulls; but they could be difficult to maneuver under power (since they sit on top of the water rather than in it), and they were likely to 'thump' in heavy seas (especially if the boat was overloaded).

An open (and rather nautical) galley with all the essentials for an extended venue was important!

It would also be hard to find a decently priced moorage (most require an end tie or have to be moored to a buoy).

We discovered that a good diesel auxiliary would cost more than a comparable gas engine; but, it was difficult not to be impressed by their economy and durability. They were also safer than a gas auxiliary.

It was important to choose a sail plan that offered a certain amount of ease and flexibility. I'd hoped to find something with roller furling, since I had no interest in securing any of our headsails in bad weather, but, for the time being, we had to settle for a boat with three hank-on jibs; and, despite an improvised downhaul, I'm still a bit tentative about scrambling forward to secure any of the headsails, especially in rough seas.

In choosing a sail plan, I definitely did not want something that was so big it might prove our undoing in a squall, nor did I want a boat that was so tender that it could not be comfortably sailed when the winds piped above 15 knots. Finally, I made sure that the main could be triple-reefed and that all sails--mizzen, main, and the three headsails--were relatively stiff with a probable remaining lifetime of at least ten years. It would have been nice to have found a boat with lazy-jacks, but none of the candidates on our short list had them, so lazy-jacks will have to stay on our "to-do" list—along with roller furling.

We eventually narrowed our search to a short list of five or six boats and began a more detailed appraisal

Here, again, we used *Yachtworld.com, Boats.com,* and *UsedBoats.com* as a reference. That way, we could specify the region we planned to visit rather than waste our time thinking about boats that were nearly impossible or too expensive to move. We also knew that the point of sale would determine where we would keep the boat, at least until her systems were checked out and she was able to assure a safe passage to her permanent mooring.

A pleasant dining area with a touch of nautical ambiance and good light was a major concern.

We assumed that we might be able to negotiate a better price if we shopped during the off-season, so we planned our visit for early January when the weather and sailing conditions were less than ideal and we might enjoy a buyer's market.

Our brokers were a tremendous help in narrowing our search. Most were quite knowledgeable, and we found that it was best to be open and forthcoming about our special interests, our intentions to shop around, and our sincerity in hoping to close a sale. We also found that it was easier to have most of the necessary financing in order before we began our search, although the majority of brokers were in a position to offer advice and help concerning expenses.

In making our final decision, we concentrated on essentials, for example, the condition of the hull, thru-hulls, sails, and standing rigging

Although first impressions can mean a lot and can give a pretty good idea about the general condition of a boat, it was important to check each boat as thoroughly as possible and not be distracted by minor problems that could easily be remedied. Thus, it was important to inspect all thru-hulls and hoses (I knew of a case where a boat sank shortly after a sale because they were defective). We also checked when a candidate was last re-rigged, since anything over twenty years old was likely to be suspect. In such cases, I noted the mast alignment and tension on all stays, made sure the swages were tight, rust free, and absent of burs; and we checked the turnbuckles to see if they were locked and rust-free. We also inspected the stanchions and chain plates to make sure that they were rust-free and water-tight. In some cases, we found that the stays had been over-tightened, possibly indicating that the boat had been stressed and raced extensively. I was reminded of a friend who bought a Catalina 27 that had been raced a good deal and whose standing rigging was badly in need of upgrades. He let his enthusiasm get the best of him, took her sailing the following day (bad idea!), and lost his mast.

We also checked the goosenecks and winches as well as the blocks, stops, and travelers; and I made sure the sheets, halyards, and mooring lines were not frayed and in need of replacement, especially since this might provide a clue about maintenance and upkeep. Finally, I checked the ground tackle and anchor winch to make sure that the anchor lines were not frayed, the chains and U-bolts were in good order, and the winch was in working order.

It was essential to know when a candidate was last hauled and inspected, when her bottom was last painted and her stuffing box serviced, and whether she had a minimum of blisters (most older boats are likely to have some—and, in many cases, too much is made of them where a few quick repairs can solve the problem). Finally, we checked the steering to make sure it was tight, and we inspected the windows and ports for water stains, which might indicate some kind of storm damage or undue stress on the hull.

The condition of the engine, electrical systems, and hull was a primary concern

The electrical systems and wiring had to be clean and orderly with no signs of jury-rigging or unsafe add-ons. We then pulled all hatches and floorboards to make sure the bilges were dry with no signs of an oil or fuel leak. I recall one boat that seemed relatively free of problems, until we discovered a major leak in her fuel tank; and another rig met most of our requirements except that the teak sole had been painted over (!), suggesting perhaps a mysterious fuel spill or some other kind of overflow. I also recall looking at an older Hunter that was certainly attractive below deck. On close inspection, however, her engine and onboard systems had a number of serious problems, and we decided that she simply wasn't the boat for us.

Next, we checked the service records and the number of engine hours since the last overhaul. This included the fuel bowl, which we checked for signs of water and dirt, and the dip stick, which we checked for signs of metal fragments or dirt (which, in the case of a diesel, was not to be confused with burnt sulphur, which blackens the oil almost immediately after the engine is started. After a simple, overall visual inspection, including a quarter berth crawl-back and bilge inspection with a flashlight, we made sure the engine started without fail and without any noticeable smoke; and we ran it for at least half an hour in gear to check for vibrations, surging, and overheating (this might be indicated by a lack of water in the exhaust, something which could indicate a defective cooling system). We also checked to make sure the oil pressure was good and the batteries were being charged and were clean and in good condition.

We tried to distinguish between essentials and simple upgrades that could be managed after we bought the boat. In the case of the boat we eventually bought (a 1970 Mariner 31 ketch), a previous deal had fallen through simply because the prospective buyer asked for so many insignificant upgrades and changes that the seller felt that it was pointless to close the sale.

Finally, it was important to survey the boat, although they are likely to vary considerably, both in detail and in cost

Although a general one or two hour survey will not provide much detail, any major problems that might have otherwise gone unnoticed might have been noted. We *did* elect to haul the boat to inspect her thru-hulls and bottom (the yard credited the expense, since-if we closed the sale-- we would be returning to refit the boat later). In some instances, it might also have been a good idea to call a rigging specialist to survey the mast and standing rigging, although it would have been impossible to thoroughly inspect the swages, since this would require an x-ray. A complete engine and transmission inspection and analysis could also reveal any hidden problems, especially if the engine had a good many hours since it was last overhauled. In fact, while the power plant on our Mariner 31 had only 500 hours, we elected to have it surveyed anyway, and the surveyor discovered a tiny, welded crack in the raw-water heat exchanger, worn bearings in the water pump, and a malfunctioning alternator and voltage regulator.

It may not always be easy to determine the relative value of a boat

Older boats are going to have older systems, and they should be evaluated accordingly. Even so, many rigs that were manufactured during the 1970's and early 1980's were overbuilt, mainly because most of the early yards did not know the durability of fiberglass. These boats were also likely to have a good deal more brightwork, since teak and other hardwoods were readily available at the time. For some, this would be a disadvantage, since they require a good deal more upkeep. For others, brightwork provides greater ambiance and beauty below deck while enhancing a boat's overall appearance above the waterline. In any case, some of the better, high quality yards were eventually driven out of business because the materials they required (including the exotic hardwoods) became too expensive and because they could not comply with federal requirements and those of OSHA. However, these yards built some excellent boats that are a terrific value even to this day. In any case, some nautical magazines such as <u>Cruising World</u>, <u>Sailing</u>, and <u>Good Old Boat</u> have some excellent articles on the prices and pros and cons of a considerable variety of pre-owned boats.

Closing the Sale

In negotiating a final price, Jeanine and I had to take into consideration some additional costs that might have been easy to overlook. First, we included the license and sales tax on our list of expenses. These we paid when we transferred the title. We also had to make sure that we had a temporary slip where we could keep the boat until we were ready to move her south to her permanent mooring (Most marinas will ask the new owner to move within a month of the sale).

Our final choice: a classic 1970 Mariner 31 ketch, *Scandia Dream*.

Fortunately, we were able to transfer temporary ownership of the slip with the boat and were thus able to avoid being put on a waiting list or paying the added expenses of a 'guest slip.' Even so, we had to pay a damage deposit, the first month's rent (most marinas charge according to the size of the slip required, not the length of the boat), and proof of liability insurance.

Sidebar:

Buying a Pre-Owned Boat: the Basics

1. Be realistic about what you can afford and what you would like: *You are not likely to find the perfect boat at the perfect price, and every candidate is going to require some kind of compromise, so be flexible about speed, size, age, the manageability of your sail plan, and short and long-term cruising comfort.*

2. Don't buy a larger boat than you can handle: *Be honest about your abilities, your reflexes and strength, your experience under sail, your knowledge of navigation and of the wind and sea, and your likely initial cruising venue; and choose your boat accordingly. Far too many* prospects have 'locked' themselves aboard a rig that they could not handle.

3. Concentrate on essentials: Look carefully at the condition of the hull and topsides and watch for signs of dry-rot, delamination, collisions, and excessive blistering. Check the condition of thru-hulls, wiring, electrical panels and fuses (including add-ons), the engine and transmission--including servicing and the date of the last overhaul, the life-expectancy of the standing and running rigging, and the condition and life-expectancy of the sails. Some additions may be essential, for example, a magnetic compass, adequate interior lighting, shore power, anchors and adequate chain and rode, safety equipment (pfd's, plugs), basic electronics (VHF, gps, depth finder, charts, flares, and fire extinguishers). You are also likely to require a dingy or tender of some sort (unless you plan to rent a slip at all times), a boarding ladder, and both a manual and electronic bilge pump.

4. Consider your cruising needs and skills: Unless you have the background and experience, avoid tender, high-tech rigs and rigs that are difficult to single-hand. Carefully inspect onboard amenities. Are they adequate and sufficiently comfortable for the size of your crew; is the head adequate? Consider the galley and stove--are they in working order and sufficient for the venues you expect to visit and the time you will be out on the water? Do you think the boat you are looking at can be managed in an emergency or maneuvered in tight quarters. Do you have the strength and reflexes to manage the sail plan; will you have, access to maintenance facilities or do you have the skills to maintain the boat--at least on an elementary level.

5. Expect additional expenses at closing: These include sales taxes, property taxes, license fees, costs of transferring the title, insurance, and mooring expenses.

Checklist: surveying a prospect

Above deck:
    A. VHF & antenna in working order
    B. Goosenecks tight, mast not warped, dented, or cracked, mast boot tight, drain holes clean
    C. Spreader lights in working order
    D. Cleats tight
    E. Windows and ports tight, no water stains
    F. Halyards, sheets not frayed or worn
    G. Blocks in working order

Deck:
    H. Turnbuckles locked, rust free, no burrs
    I. Running lights in working order
    J. Stanchions firm
    K. Deck solid, no delamination
    L. Ground tackle, chain, anchor line, anchor winch, & chuckles in working order
    M. Chain plates rust-free, no stress cracks or leaks
    N. Hatches secure and water-tight
    O. Brightwork clean, good finish, no dry rot, no scratches, worn spots in topside paint
    P. Cockpit clean, solid, no cracks or leaks
    Q. Winches in good working order

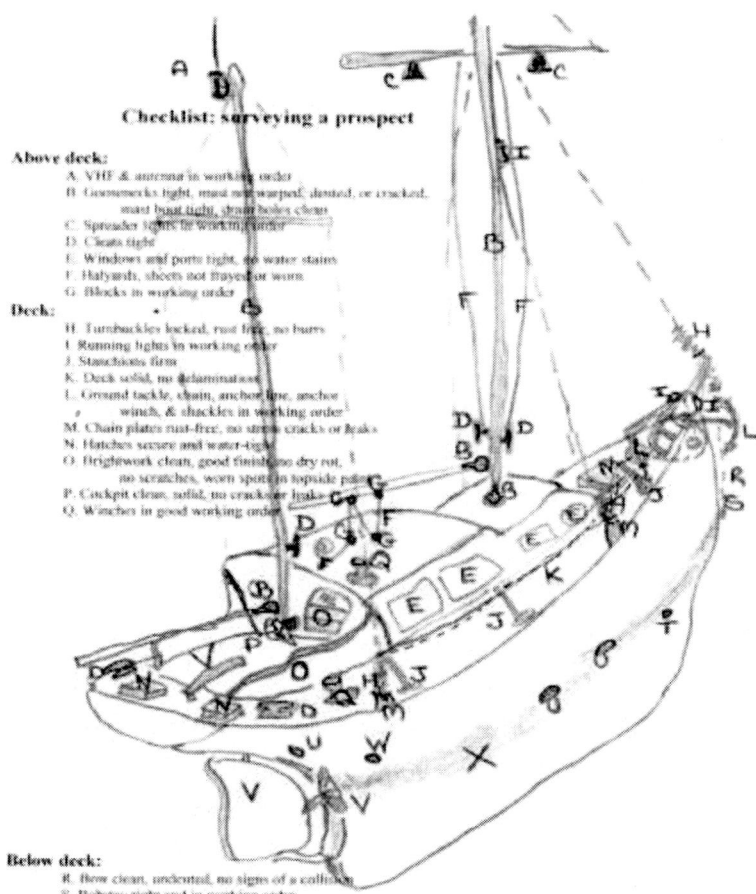

Below deck:
    R. Bow clean, undented, no signs of a collision
    S. Bobstay tight and in working order
    T. Depth-finder, speed indicator transducers in working order
    U. Thru-hulls tight
    V. Rudder, tiller/wheel tight, propeller correctly sized, tight, no warps or dents or horizontal or back and forth play in the shaft
    W. Exhaust, raw water exchange in working order (indicated by "cooling" water in exhaust, no black smoke when starting up)
    X. Bilge dry

Chapter III

The Refit

But where was the 'dream' in painting, scraping sanding, in bottom paint and dirty fuel and the mystic wizardry of electronics--what distant horizon was lacquered over in that!?

Jeanine and I were imprisoned in boatyards and practicalities and expenses without the comforting mystery of a distant horizon, a chance to go sailing, or even a glimmering sunset.

md

Anyone who buys a used car or home expects to make repairs and upgrades after closing the sale. That is simply part of the process; and--unless it is in turnkey condition--a used boat is no different. It will probably need at least a minor refit before it can be taken out.

Yes, our 'new' 1970 Mainer 31 ketch matched our needs almost perfectly: she was a proven design, in relatively good condition for her age with beautiful lines, and she was reasonably priced. Even so, while her former owners were careful about the essentials, she still needed to be hauled and refitted before her shakedown cruise to southern California. That meant that we were going to have to exercise good judgment and list our priorities with a special regard for safety, reliability, cost, and performance. For instance, even now, despite all the work we have done, we would like to add a Bimini and roller furling; but our cruising kitty is temporarily maxed out, and these extras will have to wait. In the meantime, just as every boat is a compromise between comfort and performance, every refit is a compromise among essentials, financial resources, and time available to work on the boat.

Our first priority was to make sure our Mariner was safe and seaworthy and ready to make the 400 mile excursion down the coast to her new home in Long Beach. First, we pumped out and cleaned the fuel tank, which was full of sediment and contained five to seven-year-old diesel. We also replaced the alternator and voltage regulator, replaced the cracked intake pipe on the heat exchanger, and replaced the bearings on the water pump (all as noted in the original survey).

There were a few surprises. The microphone on the VHF was broken (I should have checked it), so there was no way to transmit emergency messages. Our stern light had to be completely rewired, and the combination speed indicator and depth finder was so erratic it had to be replaced.

In addition, the external pump in the head had to be replaced, and the six gallon holding tank was much too small and had to be replaced with a larger unit.

Some of these matters were simply irritating; some were very important because they were essential to our safety and could have put us in jeopardy if they had malfunctioned when we were off Big Sur, Point Arguello, Point Conception, and windy lane during the trip south. For instance, when I first inspected the boat, I neglected to check all the running lights and only discovered the broken stern light as I prepared for our shakedown cruise. Also, had I checked the engine gauges more carefully, I would have noticed that there was no surge in the alternator when the engine was revved.

In refitting the boat and preparing her for the trip south, we decided to add a few extras of our own. In the interest of safety and reliability, we installed a second, back-up bilge pump, replaced the propane hose that ran from the exterior tank to the stove, bought a second starter battery as an emergency backup, installed a 12 volt receptacle for our hand held GPS, and had an electrician rewire one of the fuse panels and switches. We also bought a new Furuno 1623 Radar, since we would be traversing the foggy central California coast on our way south; and we bought a Uniden hand-held

VHF for use in emergencies. A new stainless steel swim ladder assured easy access to the boat if we chose to dive over the side for a quick swim and was certainly essential in case of an MOB. We also bought additional charts, an updated cruising guide, a new emergency flare kit, and new PFD's, safety harnesses, and tethers.

Since we would eventually be cruising much of southern California where fore-and-aft Bahamian moors are commonplace, we added a second anchor, a 20# Danforth with 15 feet of chain and 250 feet of 9/16 triple braid line. This supplemented the CQR, which was on about 10 feet of chain and 150 feet of 1 ½ inch hawser. I replaced the hawser with 250 feet of 9/16 triple braid, since the former was quite heavy and was so stiff and cumbersome that it was extremely difficult to stuff into the anchor well.

Although we were primarily concerned with essentials and matters of safety, we decided to add a few amenities to suit our personal tastes. Jeanine and I were interested in making the salon more comfortable and inviting, since we might be on the water for two to four weeks at a time; so we exchanged the interior lights in the salon and galley (which looked rather like something from a U-boat) for shaded lamps. We also redecorated the interior with cheerful nautical photos, decals, and the like; and Jeanine reupholstered the port and starboard salon cushions and sewed a full set of exterior cockpit cushions. We furnished the galley with special nautical dishes, bowls, cups, and glasses; and we stacked the salon with a variety of pillows and throws to make it more inviting. We also bought a shiny, brass ship's bell, a 12 inch television, an am/fm radio and cd player, and a microwave.

Our friend, Tony, checked the electrical fittings on the mast and repainted any scrapes or worn spots to minimize UV damage to the wood.

We also undertook a general clean-up of the boat, mounted a number of classic, nautical oil prints in the salon and head, repainted much of the salon, and applied teak oil to the cabin sole and interior bright work of African mahogany and teak.

Finally, we used our credit from the survey and hauled the boat to repaint both her hull and bottom. I had read a number of articles on painting and refitting, but they were generally disappointing and proved to be of very little help. In some cases, the refit as described in the magazines would have required the skills of a cabinet maker, professional painter, or journeyman mechanic. In others, I was expected to have unlimited resources in money and time—along with a perfectionist obsession that would not have permitted even tiniest flaw or mistake. This was hardly the case with Jeanine and me, since we had a limited boat kitty and had to complete all work in a little over a week, that is, unless we were content to live in a boatyard for an eternity and pay a daily storage fee that could easily reach hundreds of dollars.

Once she was out of the water, we set to work as quickly as possible and sanded and repainted *Scandia Dream's* deck, cabin, and hull with Pettit one part polyurethane enamel (which was quite easy to apply and very forgiving), repainted the water stripe and boot stripe (a soft ice blue), and sanded and refinish her bottom with Pettit Trinidad ant-foul (on sale at the boat yard). We also patched her rudder, and affixed her new name in teal-colored vinyl.

After she was splashed, we refinished the exterior brightwork (including the hatches, handrails, bulkheads, and cockpit) and repainted the rose mauling on the bowsprit. Still, I suspect that, boats being what they are, the scrubbing, varnishing, sanding, and refinishing will likely be ongoing and will never end.

I did not keep a close record of expenses. However, items which were absolutely essential ran a bit over $1,400. These included scrubbing the fuel tank, servicing the engine, repairing the heat exchanger and water pump, replacing the alternator and voltage regulator, rewiring the stern light, and installing new switches and fuse panels. bilge pumps, holding tank pump, interior lights, emergency flares, and new PFD's, plumbing, hoses, and clamps likely ran another $1,000; and navigation electronics, including the depth finder, portable VHF, and radar, probably cost another $1,400. It cost a little over $400 to haul the boat and pay for storage; refinishing her hull, bright work, and bottom cost about $300.00 (including brushes, tape, rags, and thinner); and the new anchor and rode, supplementary interior lighting, cushions, upholstery, and other amenities cost about $600. All told, we probably spent a little over $5,000 on improvements and upgrades, which still left the total cost of the boat well within our budget.

Jeanine adds a finishing touch to *Scandia Dream's* exterior brightwork.

There will be future upgrades. It is said that "BOAT" stands for *"Break Out Another Thousand"* and, given the fact that an extra thousand or so is not likely to materialize in the foreseeable future, Jeanine and I will have to wait before we can install the roller furling and Bimini--and, perhaps, a better refrigeration system (the current ice box is right next to the engine and can get very warm if the engine is run for any length of time).

Even so, we are content. *Scandia Dream* sails like a charm, is solid and seaworthy, and we think she is one of the prettiest boats in the harbor–given, of course, the fact that she would sure look even nicer with that new Bimini..

Side Bar

Managing Your Own Refit: the Basics:

Know your limits: *Let the professionals handle the critical work, especially with regard to matters of safety and performance. On the other hand, allow yourself a bit of leeway on projects you choose to complete yourself, don't be afraid to* *ask for advice, and accept the fact that minor imperfections are probably inevitable.*

Factor the size of your boat and its age:
Larger, older boats are going to be more expensive and difficult to update and refit than smaller, newer boats. As a general rule, the older and bigger the boat, the more costly and extensive the refit.

Expect a few surprises: *Even the most thorough survey is going to miss something--hidden leaks, swages with interior rust (which can only be detected with an x-ray), contaminated or rusty fuel or water tanks (which can only be seen if they are close to empty).*

Prioritize updates and refits and begin with essentials, so aesthetics, creature comforts, cosmetics, and electronic niceties may have to take a back seat while you focus on the basics.

Be realistic about how much time you have and what you can afford: *Every refit is a compromise between financial resources and wants. This means distinguishing between what must be done right away to make the boat safe and manageable and what can wait until later.*

Take a chance: *Some boats that have been neglected might be worth the trouble, the extra cost of repairs, the updates, and the time spent in the boatyard. Boat ownership isn't simply a matter of owning something that floats. It is a personal thing; and if you think you have the time, skill, and resources to refit and repair a neglected but relatively sound rig, consider taking a chance.*

Chapter IV

Finding the Right Moorage

By early spring, we were ready to move *Scandia Dream* to her permanent home. It was a daunting prospect because Southern California is one of the most popular cruising grounds on the West Coast; and, given the shortage of available moorings, most marinas are very selective about prospective tenants. They all required a credit check, proof of liability insurance (with the marina as the beneficiary), a damage deposit, and a payment history from a previous marina. Wooden boats, certain commercial vessels, and boats older than thirty-five years were often borderline; and every marina we checked had a cap on live-a-boards. However, our final choice allowed us some degree of latitude, since we live in Colorado, some 850 miles distant and couldn't just show up on a Friday evening, provision the boat, and head immediately for open water.

Moorage Rates

Moorage rates were determined by the type mooring, location, accessibility, availability, and, of course, the size of one's boat. Yachts, catamarans, and trimarans posed special problems because they usually required a side-tie, the end of a dock, or a buoy; and this necessarily limited availability. Slip rates varied considerably, although modest, out-of-the way facilities were sometimes quite reasonable and charged about a third as much as most upscale marinas and clubs. On the other hand, the more expensive slips cost as much as a small apartment, and anything over 70 feet might cost as much as a penthouse.

Types of Moorage and Security

Every moorage had a down side. Buoys were cheaper than slips, but they were vulnerable to the weather; and, given their usual isolation, access could be something of a chore. Also, long-term parking was not very good, and theft, collisions, and vandalism were always a possibility. Yacht clubs offered a dynamic social atmosphere and provided food and beverage services and reciprocal privileges with other yacht clubs. However, they were likely to be rather expensive, especially when initiation fees and monthly dues were factored in. Private residential moorings were usually in first-rate condition, but they afford very little privacy and most were rather expensive. Public docks were relatively cheap, but security was not always the best, and some were open to the public and passers-by. Private marinas, which were the most numerous, offered a variety of options; but overall quality, and essential services varied considerably. Finally, while dry storage was a viable option for seasonal boaters like ourselves and usually cost 1/2 to 1/3 the price of a slip, most had long waiting lists and did not accept sailboats over feet.

In choosing the right mooring, security was a high priority. We avoided seedy neighborhoods, unlocked facilities, or marinas and parking lots that were not well lit or did not offer 24 hour surveillance. One facility that we inspected was so dark and spooky that Jeanine would not even leave the car, even though it offered slips at a fabulous rate.

Boat traffic and congestion were always a major concern, not simply because some boaters like to trail a tsunami regardless of the location or conditions; but also because of the possibility of a collision--especially from inattentive or novice enthusiasts. This was one of the reasons we had little interest in a renting a buoy or exposed slip.

Marine operators: their perspective on costs and amenities

The marine operators we met were very helpful in pointing out the kinds of problems and concerns we might want to consider when deciding where to leave our boat. Most marinas charged by the foot according to the size of the slip or mooring buoy, and buoys were typically cheaper (and more vulnerable) than slips.

Mooring buoys such as you see here on Catalina Island in California are often congested, likely to be exposed to bad weather (especially in winter), and not particularly secure.

Some marinas and clubs had a dynamic social atmosphere; but where there was mixed use such as restaurants, clubs, and shops, we wondered if the boater's needs came first. Some of the operators asked how we planned to use our boat, because this could be a major concern in choosing the right facility. For example, some boaters might prefer a quiet atmosphere, while others might enjoy various shore-side activities with other boaters. While some boaters might use their boats on a daily basis and required quick access to their favorite cruising grounds, others like ourselves were occasional, long term cruisers where immediate access to nearby waters was not nearly as important as secure, long-term parking with easy access to shopping.

In choosing a marina, we discovered that waiting lists and slip assignment policies varied tremendously. Most facilities did not transfer a slip with the sale of a boat. This was to make sure that wait list applicants didn't have to worry about being bypassed because a slip was transferred to a new owner after the sale of the boat.

Some of the more upscale facilities offered slips with telephone, TV, and internet access; and most of the yacht clubs offered the pleasures of "camaraderie among friends with common interests, . . . and reciprocal privileges with other yachts clubs," as one yacht club manager put it.

It was generally agreed that a marina's safety equipment should include fire equipment, dock ladders, life rings, and emergency pumps. Most of the marinas we checked were members of *Clean Marinas California* which inspects marinas, lists policies regarding marina upkeep, and requires that all its employees be fully prepared for a hazmat emergency.

Maintenance, Pollution, and Long-term Dependability

We realized that, while a new or near perfect facility with a long list of amenities was going to charge premium rates, we did not want to put our boat at risk by choosing the oldest, cheapest marina available. Any facility with old docks, rotting planks, broken electrical connections and lights, an absence of locks and safety equipment, and loose or broken cleats was a guarantee of general carelessness and future problems. We were especially wary of anything more than thirty years old or marinas which might be planning to move or remodel, since there was a good chance that we would lose our slip or be asked to move during the interim.

Wildlife was going to be a problem no matter where we chose to locate. Three or four eight hundred pound sea lions can sink a boat by sleeping on the swim platform, and they are guaranteed to splotch the hull with a sticky mucus when they cough or bellow. We also learned first-hand at our point of purchase at Moss Landing that sea otters like to use a bow or bobstay to open abalone shells and the like; and seagulls were always going to be a problem, especially near public landfills and commercial fisheries.

Industrial pollution could also be a problem. Our marina at Moss Landing was located next to an estuary and a major power plant; and the particulates from the stacks and from fertilizers washing down the Salinas River left a filthy scum on *Scandia Dream's* waterline and deposited soot on her decks and cabin top. In fact, the local power company sent us a monthly check to moderate the cost of cleaning our boat.

Amenities and Accessibility

For Jeanine and me, certain amenities were absolutely essential--especially since we lived in Colorado and couldn't simply drive 850 miles, cut our lines, and head for open water. Electrical hook-ups were necessary adjuncts for charging our batteries and for short-term, dockside living; and fresh, clean water was also essential, if only to fill our tanks and wash *Scandia Dream* on occasion. We also appreciated the fact that our marina had dock carts, boat boxes, private lockers, a dingy dock, and private showers and laundry facilities. Jeanine and I noticed that some of the more upscale marinas and clubs offered swimming pools, Jacuzzis, and even tennis courts and picnic areas; but such amenities were accompanied by higher slip rates, an important consideration for anyone who lived on a pension and was looking for a secure mooring on a limited budget.

We were also lucky that our marina was close to essential services such as a fuel dock, pump-out station, and shopping mall. Also, our marina's accessibility was a major concern. Some of the locations we checked required a tedious, two day drive from Colorado, much of it on freeways and twisting two lane roads. It wasn't long before I came to appreciate the problems faced by some of the Los Angeles locals, who might have made last minute plans to go boating, only to get locked in rush hour traffic. In our case, we were lucky to find a marina that could be reached with only a moderate amount of congestion via the US-91 freeway south of Los Angeles.

Access channels varied considerably in width. *Scandia Dream* careens to starboard in reverse gear and requires a good deal of space and extra help to back out of her slip. Given a narrow entry channel, this could be especially trying, as was the prospect of a busy exit channel or harbor where the likelihood of a collision with speeding boats would have been a constant concern--indeed, this was a major downside to our Long Beach facility, which is one of the busiest harbors on the West Coast. In fact, the charts and guidebooks explicitly warn all pleasure craft (which are innumerable) to stand clear of all commercial vessels.

Scandia Dream's new home in a secure inner harbor in San Pedro, California--a modest facility with electricity, water, a boat box, locked gates, nearby shopping, and quick access to the San Pedro Channel. However, the marina's narrow access channels have occasionally been a problem, especially in a following wind.

Finally, we were interested in something relatively close to shopping, especially groceries and block ice. A nearby chandlery also proved to be helpful, since we did a lot of our own maintenance and most of our repairs. We also considered the neighborhood where we would leave our boat, especially as it related to our privacy and personal comfort. I knew of one "marina" that bordered a busy public board walk and shopping village, while another bordered a night club with live music that lasted till 2 a.m. Live-a-boards were also a concern--usually in the positive sense, since they were likely to keep an eye on our boat. On the other hand, we were curious about the number of live-a-boards at some of our prospects, especially since a couple of the more modest facilities were commonly regarded as a source of affordable housing.

A quick check of the general area surrounding the marina and the marina itself indicated something about the general character of a prospect; including the risk of fire, theft, collision, and the prevailing attitude towards boating and the sea. While it was at first difficult to discern, we were also interested in knowing if a marina had a reasonably tolerant and congenial atmosphere, both with regard to its residents and with regard to management. In one case, a resident told us that the manager was rather sullen and seemed a good deal more interested in money than in service, security, and upkeep. That was enough to dissuade us from considering the facility, even though it was ideally located.

Fortunately, in our case, we found a well-maintained, secure marina that did not bankrupt us; and, while it was somewhat out of the way, it was economical and well managed. This has proved to be a godsend; and as we spend our leisure winter hours here in Colorado, we know that our beloved ketch in California is safe and secure and ready to take us on some grand cruising adventures come next summer.

- - - - - - - -

Sidebar
Avoiding the Moorage Blues

Costs: *Don't forget to factor the damage deposit, insurance, and first and last month's rent when finalizing your moorage agreement.*
Safety: *Security should always be your primary concern. This includes the possibility of theft or vandalism, storm damage, collisions, damage from marine life, and pollution.*
Location: *Don't moor your boat where your cruising options are limited--consider where and how often you plan to go cruising and locate a marina accordingly.*
Listings: *Most regional boating publications list available moorings. You may also want to refer to the internet for a list of marinas and mooring companies in your area. Be prepared to be put on a waiting list; and, in the meantime, you may be*

forced to keep your boat at a 'guest' dock where you will probably have to pay 'guest dock' rates.

Chapter V

First Aid and Safety

Have a care where there is more sail than ballast.

William Penn

We've covered the care, refitting, and mooring of our boats. But what about us! After all, we seniors and retirees are likely to face specific issues of our own; and our special 'upkeep' and our 'refits' are just as important as our boats. So here's a bit of advice about self-care, safety, and first-aid that is absolutely essential if you hope to sail the distant horizon for many years to come.

First, if you want to live long and happily, take care of yourself, get a yearly check-up; and, if you're lucky enough to have a loving partner, listen! They'll feed you better than you'd ever feed yourself; they'll likely moderate your adventurous spirit with a strong dose of common sense; and-- despite your protests—they'll haul you to the local ER when it looks like you may not survive the night. That's why we typically outlive the loners by a country mile!

Senior Durability--Falls, Fatigue, and Heart Attacks

Most senior sailors are justifiably concerned about their durability and their declining strength, reflexes, and coordination. They worry--and rightly so--about accidents, fatigue, strokes, and heart attacks. I know people who have moved next to the local hospital so they can be rushed to the ER in the event of a catastrophic failure of some sort. It is a terrible way to live--if living it is. We should not consign ourselves to a non-life because we fear death by heart attack or stroke or some other exotic disorder. Unless your physician expressly forbids an active, moderately strenuous lifestyle, get on with your life; and don't let fear of dying keep you from living.

On the other hand, remember that you have nothing to prove anymore; and if you start to feel overly tired and short of breath, take a break, hydrate, or quit. Don't risk a heart attack or stroke because you have an obsessive completion tendency or happen to get caught up in a bone-headed marathon to prove your durability. Chronic fatigue and sleep deprivation can lead to monumental mistakes that may prove fatal. Since we are--all of us--out on the water to enjoy ourselves, there is absolutely no reason for any of us to obsess about our endurance and less than superhuman skills. Leave that to the record-setters, the Xtreme sportsters, and risk-takers. After all, most of us go sailing for relaxation and enjoyment, and that means getting plenty of rest, moderating our activities, and avoiding stress, regardless of whether we are out on the water or ashore.

Prescriptions and Medical Supplies

Before heading out on an extended cruise, arrange "vacation" refills for of all your prescriptions; and make sure that you bring *more* than enough. Sailing does not lend itself very well to scheduling. That is one of its attractions, but it also means that you should plan on an additional supply of medications if you should get holed up in a storm or your boat suffers a breakdown and you are forced to lay over for an extra week

Shipboard medical supplies ought to be limited to essentials. If you were to prepare for every possible emergency, the necessary supplies would cost hundreds of dollars. Consider what you are likely to stock in your bathroom cabinet at home, use it as a baseline, and then supplement it with the medications and dressings you might need when you're are out on the water and immediate help is not available.

Most of the popular chandleries offer a good selection of first-aid essentials for somewhere between $40.00 and $60.00--along with a waterproof kit that is thoughtfully divided into various sections according to the problem at hand, whether it be a cut, rash, fracture, burn, or bite. This will save time, since you won't have to rummage through a plethora of irrelevant items in search of essentials.

At the very least, your kit--which should be waterproof—ought to contain antibiotics such as Neosporin, Lanacane, aspirin, acetaminophen, and Ibuprofen; bandages and dressings of various sizes; surgical tapes, sterile gauze, eye wash, advanced wound closure strips, and an irrigation syringe; ointments of various sorts for bites and infections; splints, scissors, a resuscitation mask; and a ready-reference first-aid booklet. And, of course, you should know how to administer CPR and be familiar with the basics for dealing with shock, hypothermia, heat exhaustion, heart attack, and stroke.

With the exception of some insect bites, most onboard medical problems do not involve transmittable diseases, since--other than your crew--social contacts tend to be relatively limited. However, prepare your medical kit according to the size of your crew and your *current* health needs, not what you might expect some time in the future.

More serious concerns may require that you go ashore where there might at least be a dispensary, or--if you are lucky--a clinic, emergency facility, or hospital. Don't hesitate to use your cell, VHF, or SSB to call other boats or shore-side facilities if you have any doubts about a critical situation. Also, leave an itinerary of your trip with a close friend or relative, stay in touch to keep them up-to-date on your progress, and instruct them to contact the Coast Guard or local authorities if you are more than three (some say two) days overdue.

Seasickness, Sunburn, Sunstroke, and Dehydration

Seasickness is usually the most common problem among seafarers. Some of the more grizzled veterans among us may boast that they have never been seasick, but that is simply a matter of timing and luck. They might be wiser to avoid tempting fate by saying that they have not been seasick *yet*.

Pallor, cold sweats, headache, dizziness, dry mouth, lethargy, loss of appetite, and vomiting are common precursors of seasickness, although a seasick person may not present all the symptoms and not necessarily in the order listed here.

Bring the victim topside if at all possible, since stale, warm air tends to accelerate seasickness. Have the victim study the distant horizon where the sensation of rocking and the conflict between the eye and inner ear is minimized. Change course slightly if necessary and arrange for the victim to stay in the center of the yacht where rocking is less pronounced.

Ginger ale, ginger cookies, and Seven-up or Coca Cola have all been known to moderate symptoms; and a good many individuals have had good luck with a transdermal patch. Certain drugs can also be helpful, including Dramamine, Marezine, Bonine, and Antivert. Most of these medications require a lead time of at least two hours and should be taken before heading out. However, they typically result in a sleepy or inattentive crew and blurred vision.

Skin Care

Our skin tends to be a little more brittle than it used to be, so we are typically more vulnerable to cuts and abrasions. Keep a good supply of dressings handy. Rinse wounds, cuts, and abrasions with soap and water, apply Neosporin or a similar ointment, and apply a dressing. Do not let cuts and abrasions go untended, since--as seniors--we are a little more vulnerable to infection.

Sunburn is the most common skin danger, but anyone who spends a good deal of time at sea should also guard against skin cancer. UV damage and heat stroke can also be a problem, and fair-skinned, blue-eyed people should be especially careful. As seniors, our skin is no longer as resilient, so avoid long-term exposure to the sun. Its glare can be merciless, so stock a good supply of lotions and sunscreen, preferably with an SPF (Sun Protection Factor) of 15 or more, and zinc oxide (which might be applied on the nose which is extremely sensitive to sunburn). It might also be a good idea to apply extra moisturizing lotion throughout the day and especially just before bedtime.

Cool water compresses, aspirin, hydrocortisone cream, aloe vera, and Solarcaine may also reduce the pain and discomfort of a severe sunburn and moderate heat exhaustion or mild sunstroke. The risk of sunburn will diminish the longer you are out on the water, since you will gradually develop a healthy tan which will serve as an excellent barrier to the sun. Still, it may be a good idea to stock your boat with extra t-shirts, sunglasses, and a variety of wide-brimmed hats.

If you don't already have one, consider installing a bimini. Most chandleries and mail order catalogs offer a variety of moderately priced sizes and styles that can be easily installed.

Seniors don't perspire as readily as their younger sailing compatriots, so a "swim break" to minimize the possibility of heat stroke may also be a good idea. Drop your sails and kill your engine before entering the water (I know of instances where an individual suffered from carbon monoxide poisoning while in the water, and there is always a chance that your engine could accidentally slip into gear). Stay on the leeward side of the boat, so it drifts toward you as you cool off. Do not forget to suspend a ladder over the side before entering the water, and check for unwelcome sea creatures before diving in. You may also want to rinse your ears with a fifty-fifty mixture of fresh water and hydrogen peroxide after climbing back aboard.

Long term exposure to the sun and heat may also result in dehydration, heat exhaustion, and--when combined with physical exhaustion--electrolyte imbalance. Electrolyte imbalance should be of special concern to seniors, so drink at least two liters of water every day--possibly in combination with one of the electrolyte beverages such as Gatorade.

Heat exhaustion may result in lethargy and dizziness. Sweating ceases, the skin becomes hot and dry, and the victim may become delirious, suffer convulsions, and may even become comatose. It is important to reduce body temperature by immersing the victim in cool (not cold) water.

Finally, wear a good pair of dark, polarized sunglasses--preferably with dark green shading, since this will minimize glare. Your eyes can burn from the sun as readily as your skin (sometimes indicated by redness and pain). In some cases, it is even possible to be temporarily blinded, much as some skiers have suffered snow-blindness.

Hypothermia

We seniors usually have less fat and muscle to insulate us from the cold. When our bodies are unable to generate and conserve heat, the brain activates our nervous system, which reacts to the cold by constricting blood vessels and by shivering (which increases heat production), inhibiting sweat, and by increasing our blood pressure, heart rate, respiratory rate (a major concern for seniors), and our basal metabolic rate. Hypothermia (sometimes referred to as the "invisible killer") occurs when the body temperature drops below 85 degrees Fahrenheit. It is extremely dangerous.

You will have less chance of developing hypothermia if you wear extra layers of protective clothing (sweaters, parkas, caps, thermal underwear) or go below to a warmer environment. You might also try in-place exercises by stiffening and relaxing your muscles.

A quick swim over the side is an easy way to cool off. However, check for unwelcome sea creatures before diving in, don't forget to hang a ladder over the side, and stay on the leeward side of your boat.

Hypothermia can be caused by trauma, immobility, alcohol, and drugs--and, of course, exposure to cold weather or cold water. Immersion in cold water for more than an hour can result in death, even when the water temperature is in the 80's, so hang on tight in rough seas, and wear a PFD, harness, tether, and non-skid deck shoes when you are topside. If you are unlucky enough to fall into the water, the wind and sea state can accelerate hypothermia because it may be difficult to keep water out of your mouth, especially in rough seas where the wind and spray can accelerate cooling.

If you should fall overboard and it looks like it might be a while before you are rescued, assume a fetal position. Usually, your core temperature won't start to cool for at least 15 to 20 minutes, although timing may vary, depending on the water temperature. Your survival will also be determined by your body fat (more is better), your body type (tall and thin versus short and fat), your clothing (triple layers are to be preferred), your sex, your physical condition, and--of course--your age and durability.

Chest Pains

Severe chest pains are a major concern to seniors and should never be treated lightly. They may be a result of insufficient blood flow to the heart, usually because of a blockage to the heart muscle (myocardial ischemia) or a pulmonary embolism or blood clot. Chest pains may also be a result of pneumonia, emphysema, gastrointestinal disorders, muscle strain, or hyperventilation.

Fractures, Sprains, and MOB's (Man Overboard)

We seniors don't have the reflexes and keen sense of balance of our youth; and our bones are a good deal more brittle, so fractures and sprains are always a possibility. In fact, serious falls and fractures--which can result in infections and other complications--are a major cause of hospitalization.

Most people fall over the side because they stumble over deck hardware or lines or because of a misstep, a sudden, unexpected lurch, an unexpected wave, or a large wake. Such accidents are the leading cause of boat fatalities, so establish strict rules about topside safety before heading out.

The set procedure for dealing with a man overboard includes timing of the incident; marking the location of the MOB with a life ring, cushion, or horseshoe; assigning someone to point at the person in the water at all times; making a quick-stop or jibe maneuver; and initiating the recovery. For specific procedures in dealing with an MOB, see "Crew Overboard" in Chapman's Piloting, pages 92-95; pages 170-171 of the Annapolis Book of Seamanship, or pages 80-84 of Paul Gil's The Onboard Medical Handbook.

Copy one of these procedures in simplified

form and post it in a conspicuous place for immediate reference in case someone falls into the water.

To minimize accidents, install hand-holds topside and below deck; and make sure that ladders and stairs are wide, closely spaced, and forgiving with handholds for ease of descent. They should also be covered with reflective non-skid tape to minimize the possibility of a fall. Install lifelines throughout the boat, coat all decks with a slip-resistant finish, and consider installing a stern rail (as well as a pulpit) if the boat does not already have them. Life rings, slings, jack lines, and extra tethers, harnesses, and PFD's should be stowed topside; and life rings and throw rings should be secured to the stern rail and easily accessible. Inflatables should be preferred to dinghies, since they are usually impossible to capsize; and, if you have any concerns about theft, they can easily be deflated and stored topside.

Forgetfulness

Most of us are likely to have a few problems with short-term memory—in fact, it is so common that it is called *senioritus*, so don't obsess about it. Our long term memories are just fine--a bit overstocked, in fact--and short-term recall is relatively easy to deal with. Whatever it is you are trying to remember will eventually show up--perhaps a bit late, but you can be certain that it will invariably show up!

Short-term memory loss should not be confused with Alzheimer's. Everyday forgetfulness happens when you forget where you left the pliers; Alzheimer's is when you forget what they are for!

Still, it may be wise to post a check-out list to refer to when getting under way and when returning and securing the boat. Those procedures can get pretty complicated, especially on a large rig. It is all too easy to overlook a vital step, forget to open or close through-hulls, check the engine exhaust or water outlet for the tell-tale water coolant steam, unplug your shore power, and check all instruments for proper amperage, oil pressure, and engine temperature (See Appendix IV, "*Scandia Dream's* Checklist). It is also a good idea to remind yourself to check fan belts and the oil and coolant level before starting your engine, and don't forget to secure your ground tackle, mooring lines, and bumpers once you are under way. Make lists, post directions for electronics, mark your charts, bookmark important pages in your cruising guides, *and always store personal items and boat gear in the same place.* That way, they will be easier to find; but, above all, don't worry! You will probably be just fine. Everybody forgets things--it's just that we seniors are a little more sensitive about the matter.

Finally, you are less likely to overlook a step or procedure if you and your partner team up to check and double check everything to make sure that some item or procedure was not forgotten.

Vaccinations

If you are planning to cross the border or cruise in a humid, tropical climate, check with your doctor. You will likely need to be inoculated for yellow fever, cholera, malaria, tetanus, hepatitis, and typhoid fever. Prevention is always the best cure, so be careful about the water you drink (bottled water is always best). Avoid raw meats; eat only peelable fruits, and thoroughly cook all clams and oysters (ask the locals to make sure there is no *red tide* and they are safe to eat).

Diarrhea, Insects, Bites, Rashes, and Infections

Diarrhea is a possibility anytime you travel to another state or country. It can result in dehydration, which can be eased with Lomotril or Imodium and by drinking electrolytes.

Insects such as sand flies and gnats, which usually swarm in the late afternoon, can drive even the most avid sailor crazy; and, in certain areas--for example, the Channel Islands in southern California and the San Juan Islands in Washington--yellow jackets are a constant problem. Anytime you anchor offshore near a marsh, you can expect mosquitoes; so carry an insect repellant and use it liberally. We seniors have especially sensitive skin; and most insect bites, while seemingly harmless, can easily result in uncomfortable swelling, a rash, or constant itching.

Spider bites and bee stings can be moderated with an antihistamine such as Benadryl or Claritin. Finally, it might be a wise idea to check under the covers before climbing into your berth. I once suffered a nasty spider bite while pulling a mainsail out of a bag that had been stored in our quarter berth for a week or so.

Cockroaches are always a problem and usually migrate aboard in paper bags or cardboard boxes. Consider leaving boxed and bagged items in the dingy and pass cans and packages aboard individually. If any cockroaches should succeed in their migrations, use boric acid to control them, but be prepared for a cruise-long battle. Finally, check all fruits and vegetables--especially bananas--for bugs and tiny creatures such as snakes and lizards. I even know of one instance where a small monkey was found hiding among the bananas.

If you plan to go swimming, check with the

locals for any information about creatures that bite, sting, or leave a rash. Anyone over 70 is likely to be especially knowledgeable, since they have survived just about everything imaginable and can give you a pretty good idea of what to look for and what to avoid.

Be especially wary of venomous marine animals such as stingrays, scorpionfish (which usually lurk in warm waters among rocks, around coral reefs, and on the bottoms of shallow bays), certain species of catfish, hydroids, jellyfish, anemones, and certain starfish, sea urchins, and sea cucumbers. It goes without saying that sharks and other marine marauders, including barracuda, moray eels, and groupers, should also be avoided. Some seasoned sailors claim that it is safer to swim shore-side of kelp beds where there is less likelihood of encountering sharks.

Finally, be circumspect about hand-prepared foods, especially when you visit informal or outdoor cafes or food stands.

Other Emergencies

Be prepared to consult your onboard medical reference for other concerns, including shock and airway emergencies; soft tissue injuries and burns; head, neck, facial, and eye injuries; dislocations; drowning and near-drowning; and hypothermia (a serious concern for seniors) and cold water immersion (man overboard). You might also want to check the Appendix of Gil's book, <u>The Onboard Medical Handbook,</u> which deals with shock, choking, severe bleeding, chemical burns to the eye, allergic reactions, jellyfish stings, near-drowning, and hypothermia.

Finally, check to make sure that your health insurance covers you when you are out-of-state or out of the country.

Security

Far too much is made of security. If you are in a foreign country, act appropriately with respect to local customs. Dress inconspicuously; do not display large sums of money; lock away outboard motors, radios, cameras, and handheld electronics; and secure your dingy to the side of the boat, not behind it. Think twice about inviting strangers and locals aboard. It is easy enough to talk to them over the side while they are still in their dinghies, and you can easily make it clear that you don't want them aboard. If they try to come aboard anyway, be firm, meet them before they have a chance to climb over the lifeline, and direct them back into their boat.

If you have any questions about security, double lock all hatches, although they can usually be pried open within a minute or two; anchor out unless the visitor's dock can be locked, and turn on your spreader lights if you suspect that anyone is attempting to board your rig without your permission.

It is estimated that about 50% of all boats contain firearms; and, if you consider a flare gun a firearm (which it is!), then the figure is probably close to 95%. Consider whether you are *truly* capable of killing (not wounding!) an intruder and whether you are prepared to spend time in jail and go to court (a possibility in a foreign country) to defend your actions.

Possible options to a firearm or shotgun may include an air horn, which can be very effective in scaring off an intruder, or mace or pepper spray.

While the medical concerns we have discussed should in no way be taken lightly, Jeanine and I certainly do not think that they should make sailing scary or prohibitive.

Awareness, alertness, prevention, moderation, and a solid understanding of first-aid are vital; but this is true of any situation, whether ashore or out on the water.

In some ways, we are safer on the water than on the highways or even the local supermarket, where we are subject to any number of contaminants, crimes, diseases, accidents, and events involving neglect, anger, or misunderstanding. My purpose is not to frighten the reader so that he will be so horrified that he will never go out on the water, but to prepare him to be self-sufficient. Sailing and seamanship involve a plethora of finely honed skills, good judgment, and years of hard experience. Such an inventory must necessarily involve a rudimentary understanding of first-aid and accident prevention.

Medical References and Suggested Additional Reading

Chapman, Charles F. "Safety First." Chapman's Piloting: Seamanship & Small Boat Handling. New York: Hearst Marine Books, 1996. 61-113 (a solid, quick reference).

Cohen, Michael M. Dr. Cohen's Healthy Sailor. Camden, ME: International Marine, 1983.

Eastman, Peter F., M.D. Advanced First Aid Afloat. 3rd ed. Centreville, Maryland: Cornell Maritime Press, 1987 (This is a staple--essential in any ship's library).

Gill, Paul G., Jr, M.D. <u>The Onboard Medical Handbook: First Aid and Emergency Medicine Afloat,</u> Camden, Maine: International Marine, 1997 (this is Jeanine's favorite reference--simple, quick, and easy to use in an emergency!).

Rousmaniere, John. "Staying on Board." <u>The Annapolis Book of Seamanship</u>. Illustrated and designed by Mark Smith. New York: Simon & Schuster, 1989. 170-171 (Rousmaniere and Chapman are the two best references on boating and seamanship in general. Either or both should be the foundation of any ship's library—they are excellent as well for quick medical references).

Weiss, Dr. Eric A., and Michael Jacobs. <u>Marine Medicine.</u> West Marine, 2009.

Werner, David. <u>Where There is no Doctor.</u> Palo Alto, CA: The Hesperian Foundation.

Chapter VI

The Shakedown: Homeward Bound

That sail which leans on light,
tired of islands,
a schooner beating up the Caribbean
for home, could be Odysseus,....
  Derek Wolcott, Sea Grapes

For Jeanine and me, the 400 mile voyage from the heart of Monterey Bay to our new marina in Long Beach, California, was a minor epic, especially since we would have to skirt the rugged Central California Coast--including Big Sur, Point Arguello, and Point Conception, and run down Windy Lane, bound for Santa Barbara, the San Pedro Channel, and Hurricane Gulch, which was just west of Long Beach. It was a daunting prospect, although I expected something of a sleigh ride after we made Point Conception and the wonders of Windy Lane. Perhaps we might even be free to sail in an idyllic neverland of perfect wind and sea while indulging in the pleasures of a warm southern California sun. Such were our prospects for the second half of our Odyssey—excepting, of course, the wonders of Hurricane Gulch.

In the meantime, we were stuck at Moss Landing and we were frustrated. The harbor itself, the nearby towns of Castroville, Monterey, Salinas, and even the outlying bay were wrapped in a cold, unrelenting fog that refused to burn off, even by late afternoon. Still, we were not to be dissuaded and waited patiently like a cat at a mouse hole.

On the morning of the fifth day, the fog began to lift; the sun burst through the haze; the sky turned a soft, baby blue; and the sea sparkled with diamonds.

We had a brief window and no time to waste. I locked down the car (I would return later by train to retrieve it), and we cut our lines, made for the breakwater, hoisted the jib and main, and headed southwest, bound for Monterey. *Scandia Dream* took the bone in her teeth and ran merrily up the bay, heeling only slightly in the rhythmic spray and gurgle of the sea rushing past. As I raised the mizzen, the windward pressure on the tiller eased, and *Scandia* steadied even more.

Any apprehension we might have had about banging over the sea with so much canvas aloft dissolved like the morning fog, and we knew that we had at last fulfilled our dream and had found the perfect boat. This, we thought, is about as close to heaven as we might get in this life. In fact, we almost felt a little guilty for having so much fun. It seemed as if we were a couple of escaped felons as the breakwater slowly disappeared in our wake, and two hours later, the entire bay was bathed in sunshine, all except for the marina at Moss Landing, which was again wrapped in a thick, fuzzy cloud of fog.

We rented a berth in Monterey and celebrated our giddy escape by dining out. We had entered a whole new world; Monterey was beautiful and clean and clear; the hot showers at the marina were a luxury; and we spent the entire evening babbling and grinning about our escape and the journey to come.

Later that night, we took one last look at our charts and cruising guide and decided that we should traverse the Central Coast and Big Sur the following night when conditions were most favorable. That would put us in San Simeon shortly after sunrise when there was enough light to find a safe anchorage.

At about 1700 the next evening, we cut our lines and headed west, making our way past a large flotilla of sailboats that was clustered together in a Wednesday night beer can race, past the largest of them as they headed back to the marina, past the last vestiges of Monterey, and westward into the evening fog until we were completely alone, a very small boat in a blind nether-world whose barely distinguishable light was suffused in a filmy, orange, sunset haze. By the time we turned and headed southeast past Pt. Pinos, it was completely dark. Above, in the thickening haze, our mast light was barely discernible, and our red and green running lights glowed dimly off the bowsprit and crumpled jib. Beyond the cockpit, the only visible evidence that we were moving was the gentle rock and sway of the boat on a glassy sea, the sound of the engine, and the slight ripple and foam from our wake directly and barely visible over the side. We felt like a spaceship, an alien visitor bumping south through an opaque sea, the Central Coast showing eerily in black on the radar some sixteen miles to the east. We might as well have been on Mars—no, perhaps entangled in the atmosphere of Venus, thick, oppressive, pervasive as it was.

It got colder as the night passed on. Point Sur came up on the radar, matching my charts in profile, then Pfeiffer Point. The night chill was penetrating and inescapable. I pulled on a second turtle neck and then a third and then every sweater I had and my ski parka besides, and I was still cold. Jeanine brewed a second pot of coffee; and we droned south into the gloom. I was grateful for the absence of wind and wary of the engine, whose temperature hung precariously at 190 F, even at 1600 rpm. Shortly before 0400, the moon rose and hung above the fog. I used it to maintain my heading by centering it between the mizzen stays. This was something of a relief, since I had spent the last twelve hours tiller staring at the GPS and radar, and it had been nearly impossible to maintain a constant heading; indeed, I sometimes wandered off course by as much as five degrees, and only the land shift on the radar screen warned me that I was running too far east or west.

By 0600, the sun had risen through the fog; and, as the crescent moon faded, I took bearings with the sun. My course was no longer so erratic; and the dawn light was something of a relief from the ghostly blue and yellow glow of the GPS and radar, my only light for the previous twelve hours.

We reached San Simeon by mid-morning, but the offshore fog hadn't lifted, and I could not find the entry buoy, not even when my GPS indicated that we were less than a quarter mile from the beach. We gave up rather than risk putting *Scandia Dream* on the beach, and headed for Morrow Bay thirty miles south. It had a Coast Guard station; and, if the channel proved too dangerous to make on our own, we could probably hail them to guide us in. Even so, Morrow Bay was another five hours, and that meant we would have been at the helm for more than twenty-three hours. Strangely enough, I was not very sleepy, perhaps because of all the caffeine and adrenalin in my system.

Morrow Bay was socked in despite the early afternoon sun; and we called the Coast Guard to guide us to a safe haven.

They had one other boat before us (it seems that we weren't the only ones who had been stranded in the fog). I gave them our coordinates, and they promised to be out in less than ten minutes. I ran in circles for the next six or seven minutes, and then they broke through the gloom, a massive, steamy, rumbling grey vessel with a Christmas tree mast full of navigational goodies and a jubilant crew of young men with the supreme self-confidence of youth and a touch of good humor as they guided us to safety. Half way into the harbor, we slowed to let a whale pass; and then we made our way to the security of a guest mooring at the Morrow Bay Yacht Club, while our guide headed back out to escort another lost soul to safety.

Later that afternoon, we visited the clubhouse and were peppered with advice on our passage to Point Arguello and Point Conception. It was generally agreed that we should make our way some thirty miles farther south to Port San Luis before making a run at the infamous Cape. Timing was of the essence; the weather could change in a heartbeat; and, if conditions were favorable, we needed to be close by and ready to go.

The next day, we made Port San Luis, parked on a buoy for the remainder of the day, congratulated ourselves on our passage through Big Sur, and checked the weather. Since the Cape would probably be most favorable at dawn, we planned to leave San Luis sometime around midnight. We first thought we would lay over an extra day, but I happened to check NOAA weather shortly before midnight; and conditions were simply too promising: the winds at Point. Conception: NW 15-20, wind waves 4-6 feet; for the following day, NW winds increasing 30-35, wind waves, 10-12. A window of opportunity had opened, if only briefly; and we had to take advantage of it, or there would be no way of knowing how long we might have to wait before we had another chance.

I woke Jeanine, we dressed hurriedly, released *Scandia Dream* from her mooring buoy, wound our way through a tangle of darkened yachts and buoys, made our way past the Unocal Oil Pier, and headed southwest into open water, Point Sal,

Purismo Point, and the Cape.

The seas were glassy and a horribly lumpy, but we were in good shape. Our little ketch was settled and solid, and our engine temperature dropped to a more comfortable 185 as we headed for the two desolate and formidable headlands that serve as a kind of informal boundary between the central and southern coast.

Point Conception and Point Arguello constitute an abrupt outcropping that lies directly in the path of unobstructed northwest winds, and this results in unstable air, a good deal of lifting, and a terrific "venturi" effect that funnels the wind into the open sea. I planned to maintain a heading about 10-12 miles offshore to minimize the "venturi"; but, as we approached Point Arguello, the sun disappeared in a veil of clouds, the sky turned gray and dismal, and off the to the west, a tumult of storm clouds pushed against the chaotic sea and shoved wave upon wave against the building swell. I had a foreboding that we might have to deal with an afternoon gale and hoped to round Point Conception before it struck. That would put us in the lee of the point with the wind at my back.

As we made our way past Arguello and altered course for Pt. Conception, the sea grew wilder and slammed against our beam ends. The chop started to build, the wind piping from the northwest, the wind waves breaking against the lazarette. I hoisted the jib to stabilize the boat and kept the engine at a steady 1600 rpm, but it wasn't long before we were surrounded by vicious white caps that slammed against our transom and shoved us southeast with increasing momentum. The larger swells passed through us, bound eastward with unrelenting power, our speed slowing to 5 ½ knots as we were pulled to the crests; and, then, we plunged downward into the ever-widening troughs, surfing past 8 knots, and then 9, our billowing foresail tracing the curvature of our mast against the gray sky, the breaking crests nipping at our stern, but, they never broke over *Scandia's* transom. About a quarter mile to the south, a large Beneteau plunged north under a reefed main, three tiny men seemingly perched on her windward rail, her bow lifting high out of the water only to slam into the troughs in a hail of spray. I wondered if they were laughing or howling and wished them Godspeed. As we headed past the infamous lighthouse some fifteen miles to the north, I spotted a pod of dolphins, then another, and another, and then we were surrounded by dolphins, bounding and diving as if choreographed in a union of twos and threes, sometimes rolling out of the sea to inspect our bow before disappearing into the depths.

And so the morning wore away, *Scandia Dream* pulling at her helm, the wind increasing to a buzz in the rigging, while the waves nipped at our transom and pounded over the bowsprit. It was a sleigh ride, but I had been at the helm for more than nine hours and was exhausted. My prime concern was to make Santa Barbara, another forty miles down the coast before late 106afternoon.

Jeanine relaxes after a brief shopping spree on State Street in Santa Barbara before being whisked off to perhaps the most romantic restaurant we have ever visited.

Only then would we be able to take life at a more leisurely pace. We continued on; a pilot whale joined us, showing his dorsal, paralleling our course for at least half a mile; and then he was gone.

We made Santa Barbara by early afternoon, checked in with the harbor master, found our assigned berth, and spent a full day resting–I had been at the helm over eighteen hours, but Santa Barbara proved irresistible. We spent the next three days wandering the shoreline and lovely parks at our leisure, did a bit of shopping and dawdling on State Street, and dined in the most intimate Italian restaurant I have ever known.

By the third day, we were ready to move on, running headlong down Windy Lane with a terrific wind at our backs, bound for Channel Islands Harbor under full sail, enjoying the full, guiltless pleasures of sunny, summer, southern California cruising. We laid over for a few days at the Anacapa Isle Marina in the Channel Islands Harbor near Oxnard, lounged at pool side, and took full advantage of the southern California warmth and hospitality. Another day, this one a bit longer, brought us to Marina Del Rey west of Los Angeles and the warmth and hospitality of the Pacific Mariners Yacht Club, arguably the most congenial collection of sailors and humorists that I have ever met.

The next day, we made the run across to the Isthmus on Santa Catalina Island, passing through the channel with both mizzen and jib, "Scandia Dream" taking the bone in her teeth in all her glory–it was a grand sail. The sea sparkled in the wind, the sun was full, the skies blue–a celebration of the tumult of wind and water, and *Scandia* tipped her bows and danced the afternoon in wind and spray and in the rock and sway of the sea. We arrived at Two Harbors at dusk and enjoyed a perfect sunset just as the wind piped to about 20. knots.

Scandia Dream rolls with the swells at the entrance to the Isthmus on Santa Catalina Island. The following day, we pulled our anchors and rented a buoy in the inner harbor.

We dropped all sails and anchored just north of Isthmus harbor, but an offshore wind kept us broadside to the swells the entire night, and we clunked back and forth in our berth like a couple of logs on a blanket.

We never slept a wink, and the following morning, we elected to head farther into the harbor where the wind and the swells could not find us. For the next two days, we relaxed, barbecued steaks, and took our leisure poking around the village and the Isthmus, wandering the path to the south side of the ocean where the island opened up on the grand Pacific that stretched far away to the west.

The next afternoon, we struck for Avalon, a kind of California chic-Mediterranean-Mexican town with a truckload of fancy restaurants and hotels and a weird, southwest mix of charm and mercantile clumsiness.

We slept like happy puppies beneath the moon with the hatch open, and struck Long Beach the following day, the winds from the Northeast pulling us homeward with increasing velocity until our decks were soaked, and Jeanine had to shut and lock all our ports.

I dropped the main only when Jeanine had enough (and made *that* very clear), then the mizzen, and finally, just as we passed the Los

Angeles light, the jib.

Hurricane Gulch had done her best to make sure we enjoyed the final ride into the bay, and we followed a massive containership toward our berth, making our way past a series of breakwaters until it lay just ahead of us. I set out the bumpers, docked smartly, tied the lines, and Jeanine and I stepped onto the dock.

We had arrived and made it, safely with a bundle full of memories to commemorate our shakedown Odyssey. The sea had taken the measure of us, shown us her power and wonder, and *Scandia Dream* had performed well. Now, in her new home, she was berthed only in preparation for the next journey, the next bewildering pilgrimage, perhaps back north to Santa Barbara and the Channel Islands, perhaps back to Santa Catalina, perhaps south to Dana Point, San Diego, and Ensenada. Come late fall and next spring, who could tell what marvelous pleasures and sublime wonders lay before us. All we knew as we tied the last of *Scandia's* mooring lines was that the ocean lay sublime and wonderful just to the north and south of us; and we had only to loose our lines, head for open water, and we would be on our way.

That was a wondrous prospect.

Chapter VII
Sailing at Seventy

There are no simple formulas, no quick answers--we must find our own way; for we have, each of us, a separate pact with heaven and the distant horizon

md

I just celebrated my seventieth birthday; and, while it is natural to wonder how many more birthdays I have yet to enjoy, I am just as concerned about the quality of my life and how long I can continue to go sailing and do the things that make me happy. Being older certainly has its advantages: the iota of wisdom, the new-found serenity and gentler life style, the joy of loving overmuch. Of course, I don't have the same reflexes and durability that I enjoyed some twenty years ago, and I have had to take a good, hard look at my passion for sailing, the opportunities that still lie before me, and the horizons I must eventually forgo.

A very good friend who is much older than me once said that we must eventually renounce the things we love most. There can be little doubt that any kind of finality, no matter how great or small, can be terribly difficult, regardless of how stoic the perspective or how great the justification. On the other hand, when I look at my own prospects, I suspect that the very best is yet to come, although my values and interests have undergone a remarkable change since Jeanine and I bought our first boat many, many years ago. We no longer have much interest in long passages, nor do we care about testing our mettle in rough seas or gale force conditions. While our familiarity with danger has made us braver and more circumspect, it has also made us less daring, perhaps because we've had too many lucky escapes, perhaps simply because we now sail to *enjoy* ourselves, not to blunder through storms, race with other boats, or push ourselves to the limit in some marathon endeavor that might test our durability.

So long as we do go out on the water, we know that we should expect the unexpected, and we know from personal experience that stress, fatigue, and over-exertion can result in accidents, serious injury, or even worse. We are deeply concerned about safety, and seamanship; we pay close attention to the weather; we avoid unnecessary risks; and we leave a copy of our itinerary with our marina and with family members. We also make sure that our boat is in good condition and capable of handling a sea, and this includes a careful check of all equipment, including our sails, rigging, ground tackle, engine, thru-hulls, electronics, and emergency equipment.

So why then do Jeanine and I love the water and why do we hope to continue sailing for a good while yet to come?

It is a deeply personal thing and has a lot to do with our profound kinship with the natural world and the remarkable sense of personal freedom when we set out for a distant venue. You see, if Jeanine and I choose, we can hoist sail and chase the sun until it falls into the sea; we can contemplate a moonrise on a quiet evening, or we can spend a week of luxury in a cozy anchorage reading and napping with only the ebb and flow of the tide and the sound of rustling waves to break the stillness.

Perhaps we simply love sailing because of the sanctity of wildness, or perhaps—and this is especially important—it lies in the most intimate possible connection of the natural world and the wonder of things perfect and eternal—a possibility that is especially important to Jeanine and me. Like the seagull who is rocked to sleep among the ever-rolling waves, we may even discover our unrecovered innocence in the ebb and flow of a distant truth and the immutable pleasure of total freedom.

There has always been something beautiful and sublime about sailing; even the homeliest of boats is a thing of wonder when under sail, but given the terrific variety of sailboats, of high-tech racers, weekend cruisers, day sailors, luxury yachts, family trailerables, and the like, Jeanine and I have our preferences; and, while just about any boat will require a bit of maintenance now and then (upgrades and refits are an inevitable part of boat ownership), we have no intention of losing our perspective on refits and upgrades in perpetuity, especially if the weather is grand, the wind is perfect, and we could be out sailing. Too much boat work and too many refits can be a constant distraction from the joy of sailing; and we know first-hand that it is all too easy to get enthralled by the prospect of a picture perfect rig at the cost of getting out on the water.

I knew a rather quiet, mild mannered old gentleman who had once been a carpenter by trade. Year by year, he had applied his every skill to the beautification of a lovely Catalina 36 that was obviously his first love. But time had passed him by with barely a glance; and he had become so obsessed with sandpaper and varnish that by the time he was *almost* ready to go sailing, he couldn't. He was simply too old and too fragile to manage the boat alone; and so he wandered the dock in a kind of confused reverie, spent his afternoons sitting forlorn and alone in the cockpit of his beloved boat, and waited for those rare occasions when his grandchildren might come down to the dock and take him out for a sail.

Of course, I recognize that it is inevitable that Jeanine and I will eventually have to evaluate our own sailing prospects, no matter how difficult or painful. The consequences of evading a hard reality check are unthinkable, and better a pro-active concern than the horrors of an accident at sea. I remember talking with an elderly gentleman up in Seattle whose family had insisted that he was too old to go sailing anymore. He had become forgetful, and it was simply a matter of time before he hurt someone or lost his boat. After a long and agonizing discussion, they felt that they had no choice but to insist that he sell his boat, a gorgeous 47 foot Hans Christian that could have gone anywhere in the world. When I saw him, he was waiting quietly in the cockpit while his daughter signed the final papers before taking him home; and I could tell he was on the verge of tears. Perhaps he was at the end of his days, perhaps not; but it was a terrible reminder of the crippling uncertainties that will ultimately and irretrievably beset us all, regardless of our hopes and passions. I think that is why Jeanine and I would like to keep both the trailerable *and* the blue water ketch. *Scandia Dream* is in one regard the perfect retirement boat. She is exceptionally stable, easy to sail with a minimum of add-ons and sail adjustments, and she is loaded with a host of creature comforts and amenities. However, she is somewhat hefty, almost forty years old, and rather costly to maintain. Our trailerable, *Lady Jeanine,* is extremely versatile, easy to manage, economical, and very responsive, although both rigs need electric anchor winches, so I won't have to suffer terminal exhaustion hauling the cursed anchors to the surface; and *Scandia* is going to need roller furling, so I won't have to teeter from the bowsprit while dousing the jib in a sea. Other than that--and perhaps an extra handhold in *Lady's* entry hatch, Jeanine and I are pretty well set--providing I can figure out an easier way to provision and store our gear, especially on the trailerable.

Jeanine and I have been life-long sailors and boating enthusiasts; and we dearly hate to give it up. Both the sea and the inland canyons and lakes are so beautiful; and, today, the mere prospect of being out on the water and expanding our horizons is sufficient to fulfill any passion I might once have had when I drove before gales and hoped to make my way into the record books. Now, I just want to celebrate the rock and sway of the sea, run with the west wind on a well-found boat, and chase the stars until they fall beneath the horizon. The voyage itself and the untold wants by land can only be satisfied in an occasional escape to the scattering spray, a steady helm, and the sun gleaming bright on our sails. Perhaps life is at its fullest when we can wander gypsy-like before the wind with only the waves and the singing of the mew and the clamor of gannets to keep us company.

There are many dimension to this remarkable business of sailing. Regardless of whether it involves a few hours day-sailing, a weekend cruise, or the heart-felt pleasure of a month-long venue, I am certain that Jeanine and I will never quite relinquish our love of the water and the wind and the stars; and, so long as we can hoist a sail without undue discomfort and stress, we will likely continue sailing as long as we can drive a car. We also know that, where additional creature comforts and conveniences are possible, sailing can be even more enjoyable, most especially if the venues are pleasurable, the wind is steady, and our boat is as well-suited to our dreams as the immutable, chalk blue sky overhead.

Appendices
* * * * * * * * *

Appendix I:
A Note for Novices

Some of you are just starting out. Perhaps you've always dreamt of an untethered life: a boat of your own; new, unimaginable horizons; sea-born sunsets; and not a care in the world. You may have even lingered overlong at the water's edge and watched the sailboats play in the wind, or you spent an afternoon sailing with a friend and marveled at the silence or the gentle rock of the waves.

It sounds easy enough, and it's partly true; but, if you've never owned a boat or sailed alone, I'd like to offer some advice--just to make the dream a little easier.

First, learn from an experienced sailor, attend a sailing school, or look for a sailing club. Sailing is both simple and complicated. You can learn basics in a few hours; the fundamentals take a few days; the rest will take a lifetime. Check the ads in sailing magazines like <u>Cruising World</u>, <u>Sail</u>, <u>48 North</u>, or <u>Sailing</u>. They list a host of sailing schools, and most are certified by the American Sailing Association, which has more than 300 plus schools worldwide (www.asa.com). Another option is the "Offshore Sailing School," which has been in business since 1964. You can find them at (www.offshoresailing.com/sail). Also check " 'J' World" if you're interested in performance sailing (www.jworldschool.com). If you live near any sizable body of water, there's probably a sailing club nearby. Most offer memberships at a reasonable rate.

It's even possible to learn solely from a book. Study hard, wear a PFD, stay clear of traffic, and choose a safe (and small) body of water for your first excursion. I started out with an eighteen foot boat at the age of thirteen, a book in one hand and the tiller in the other.

Take baby steps. Learn the vocabulary of sailing and practice the basic knots (square knot, cleat knot, bowline, slip knot, half hitch). You should probably start small. Small boats are very forgiving, easy to maneuver, and won't do much damage if you make a mistake. However, they're also very tippy and easily founder. On the other hand, while big boats have a lot more stability, they can wreak havoc and are very dangerous in the hands of a novice.

Regardless of your preference, keep everything simple and stick to the fundamentals. Above all, stay away from the slick racers and high tech wonders.

Our '16 Man 'O War was fun to sail, but about as stable as a bud vase. A great lake sailor, she was almost impossible to damage, weighed less than 600 pounds, and was easy to tow and launch.

As for matters of comfort and safety, it's just about impossible to cover everything in a primer like this, but here are a few items to keep in mind:

1. Just as most powerboats are meant to tip

fore and aft with the bow up in the air, sailboats are meant to tip left and right (port and starboard). Don't be alarmed; they're *supposed* to do that! In fact, they don't do very well with the mast straight up. Ten, fifteen, even twenty degrees are okay on a monohull. It just seems a little weird at first. Sometimes, a boat that tips too far (30-45 degrees) will even dump its sails and turn into the wind--all on its own. Of course, that doesn't always happen. Very small boats could swamp or founder, but they're not likely to sink. Some will eventually turn turtle with the mast pointing into the depths. If you can swim to the centerboard before this happens, you can right the boat by standing on it.

As you might have guessed, narrow boats tip (heel) more than broad ones; boats with tall masts tip more than fractional rigs and ketches (ketches are so stable they were once used to launch mortars). Although it is fairly easy to right a sailing dingy or laser, righting a small catamaran is slightly more challenging and requires the use of a halyard. Some cats even top their masts with a large ball to keep them from flipping upside down

2. Sailboats are locked to the laws of nature. Their behavior is determined by wind and the waves. Learn to watch the water and keep an eye on the sky at all times. The surface of the water will tell you about the wind--where it's coming from

and how much (breaking waves indicate winds of ten knots or more). If you're sailing offshore on a coast of any size, don't confused rollers with wind waves. Most rollers are just big, harmless hills-- until they break against the shoreline.

Never, under any circumstance, sail close to a beach with a breaking surf.

3. Make sure that your boat is in good condition before heading out. Test and check the motor and auxiliary tanks thoroughly. Allow for sufficient fuel, check all through-hulls, make sure bilges are dry, check your gauges if you have an onboard auxiliary, and secure all lines properly. If you are planning an extended trip or if you sail a larger, more complicated rig, post a checkout list and follow it (See, for example, *Scandia's* checklist, Appendix V)

4. If this is your first time out, learn how your boat behaves--even if you have taken lessons. What is its turning circle? How does it respond to the helm? Fin keel boats can turn in a very tight circle; shoal keel rigs need a lot of space. How does it back? Shoal keel boats don't back very well under power and usually walk to port or starboard, depending on the prop. How quickly does it tack? Will you have to "back" the jib to swing the bow completely around? If your boat has an outboard motor, use it to tighten your turning circle in close

quarters. Know your boat's "draft" and navigate accordingly. Shallow areas and shoals are typically indicated by light blue water. Breaking offshore waves usually indicate a hazard that is close to the surface.

    4. Always wear a PFD. Wear a safety tether in heavy weather and clip it to a stanchion or cleat when you are more than a mile offshore and plan to leave the cockpit. Do not clip it to a lifeline. Some sailors prefer to wear them at all times, regardless of the conditions. Larger boats should always carry an emergency boarding ladder, a life ring or horseshoe, and fire extinguishers.

    Consider which electronics are essential. If you will be sailing any distance offshore, carry a cell phone and stow flares. Larger boats should also be equipped with a VHF and GPS. Radar may be helpful if your cruising grounds are heavily trafficked or if fog is common. Finally, a good set of charts is absolutely essential.

    5. If you are a novice or this is your first time out, check the conditions. The wind should be no more than ten knots (slightly breaking waves). Double check all lines to make sure that they are properly coiled and free of knots. Pay special attention to halyards and sheets, which tend to jam or cross each other, especially the halyards.

    Paddle or motor away from the dock or beach.

Leave plenty of distance between your boat and the shoreline. Turn the boat in the direction of the wind. Wrap the leeward jib sheet clockwise around the winch and secure it. Hoist only the main; or, if you have a roller-furled jib release it about one third. Turn the boat slightly downwind and winch the jib until it is flat along the luff (the part of the sail facing the wind). When it stops billowing, your sail is (almost) perfectly adjusted. Test your helm. How does the boat respond? Watch how the sail behaves. When you think you have the boat perfectly under control, head up into the wind, secure the sheet, and hoist the remaining sail. Repeat the process. Pull the sail in a bit and turn the boat so that the wind pushes at the sail from the side--neither directly astern nor 45 degrees off the bow. You are now on a "reach." Winch in both sails until they stop luffing. Prepare for your return trip. Turn into the wind and winch in both sails. Note how the boat is tips (heels) the closer you steer in the direction of the wind. It is unlikely that you will be able to head more than 45 degrees off the direction of the wind. Thus, if your destination is straight ahead, you will have to zig-zag or "tack" back and forth to get back to your destination. Plan your trip accordingly. If you are uncomfortable, roller furl the jib about half way. If you are struck by a sudden gust, head the boat in the direction of the wind and force the sails to luff or even flog a bit. Watch your sails, and be prepared to make these corrections so you won't founder. Learn to use telltales (strips of ribbon hung from your stays and the leech of your sails). They will indicate the direction of the wind. When your sails are properly adjusted, the telltales on your sails should *all* fly straight back.

Notice that a sail works exactly like the wing of an airplane, only it is vertical instead of horizontal. That is why a sailboat is "pulled" along, just as an airplane is "held" (not pushed) up when it flies.

Always be on the lookout for hazards, other boaters, and changes in the wind and waves. Watch the horizon for changes in the wind? Are the waves getting larger? Keep track of neighboring boats: where are they and what are they doing. Study the 'rules of the road' and obey them, as you would follow the rules as if you were driving a car. *Never give another boater directions* (you could be wrong and you could be liable for damages as well).

In any case, always assume that other boaters do not know the rules of the road or are not paying attention. Never challenge another boater, even when you have right of way. Use your horn properly to signal your intentions. In most cases, one short blast means "I intend to overtake you on your starboard side: two short blasts mean "I intend to overtake you on your port side." If the overtaken vessel agrees, it responds in kind. If the overtaken vessel disagrees or is in doubt about the safety of such a maneuver, it sounds a danger signal: a minimum of five short blasts.

7. Test "stopping" your boat by facing into the wind and then falling off the wind to regain forward momentum. If you are under sail with the wind at your back, learn how much of a turning circle you will require to spin the boat around and into the wind to bring it to a stop beside the dock. Be wary of the boom. When you turn with the wind at your back, it will swing over the cockpit with terrific force. Do not get caught in its path: it could knock you over the side or, at the very least, hit you hard or even knock you unconscious.

If you have auxiliary power, start it before dropping your sails (to make sure it starts). Drop your sails a good distance from the dock, and approach your mooring *very* slowly. Never race up to a dock, whether under sail or under power.

8. Study your books and don't be afraid to ask others for advice. Learn how to reef your sails, anchor, navigate, read a compass, triangulate, and read charts. Chapman's <u>Piloting</u> and Rusmaniere's <u>The Annapolis Book of Seamanship</u> are your two best references--next to your simplified "how to

sail" book.

9. Learn how to anchor properly--study anchoring etiquette and learn the principles of safe anchoring from Chapman's or Rusmaniere.

10. **Never:**

a. Sail at night until you have gained considerable experience under sail and understand all the nuances of navigation.

b. Sail distances in excess of fifteen miles without a compass (at the very least) and charts.

c. Sail without a life ring and PFD for all crew members.

d. Invite more guests than the boat is certified to carry.

e. Lose control or your boat, panic, or get lost. Make note of all landmarks, even on short day trips. Plan every cruise accordingly.

f. Take chances of any sort. Leave the risk-taking to fools and skilled professionals.

Appendix II

Heavy Weather Tactics

Anyone can hold the helm when the sea is calm.
Publilius Syrus Maximus

Of course, the first rule for any boater, large or small, is *if in doubt, don't go out.* In other words, if the weather looks bad, stay put.

Second, if something goes wrong or you have doubts about a situation, don't just sit there and fret; do something about it.

Sail and hull management

If at all possible, run on a broad reach with the wind. Hoist a fully reefed main and pull it in as much as possible to avoid being overpowered. If your jib has roller furling, do not let it out more than a foot or two, since headsails are difficult to control in a gale. In any case, your object is to heel the boat to leeward very slightly (sailboats are not designed to run fully upright) so that overtaking waves splash off you boat where the transom and windward hull meet.

Engine management

If you decide to motor sail and have an outboard motor, make sure that it is tightly clamped to the transom. More than one engine has had a clamp break loose, resulting in no end of trouble. Motor sail under a fully reefed main at about 3/4 throttle to avoid engine fatigue. If the propeller cavitates, pull back on the throttle immediately; then slowly bring the engine back to speed. Calculate your fuel reserves carefully, and do not risk running out of fuel, since this could leave you dead in the water. Keep a gallon jug of water and a fire extinguisher close at hand when refueling the utility tank.

If you do not have enough fuel to bring you to a safe harbor, shut down your engine, hoist sail, and restart your engine only when you are close enough to power safely into the entry channel and your dock.

If you have an inboard engine, consider whether it might be to your advantage to motor sail, heave to, or reef and run with the wind. Keep a constant eye on your engine temperature, oil pressure gauge, and amp meter. If they indicate any problems or if you smell anything funny, have your partner check all hoses, fuel lines, shut-off valves, cables, and fan belts. It may be something as simple as a broken fan belt, clogged thru-hull, or clogged filter.

Safety equipment

At the very least, you should have a VHF, a life ring or horseshoe, and a life sling. Keep the VHF turned on at all times and monitor channel 16 and NOAA weather hourly for updates on the weather. A dingy should be immediately available. If you decide to tow it rather than bring it aboard, use two short painters (to avoid fouling your propeller) in case one of them should fail, and make sure that it is fully inflated and the oars are secure. You may have to decide which is safest: dragging it or stowing it aboard (will it fly off with a gust; is your boat so small that it will be nearly impossible to reach if you store it on the bow?).

If you get caught in a lightning storm, do not touch stays, cables, or chain plates. Some experts suggest connecting jumper cables to your stays and dangling them over the side to ground the boat, but the jury is out on this strategy because a grounded boat may attract a strike. In any case, your engine, which is connected to your batteries and, hence, your electronics, already provides some grounding, so there is no way that you will be fully insulated anyway.

Store your wooden plugs, PFD's, flares, safety harnesses and tethers, flashlights, and, if possible, your foul weather gear where they are readily accessible. Make sure that anyone who goes topside is clipped to a jack line (lifelines are not sufficient) or a mooring cleat. Stow vital personal items and documents in a special, watertight container or ditch bag and keep sweaters, parkas, and caps, and gloves on hand to avoid hypothermia, since it can lead to exhaustion and impaired judgment. A thermos of coffee or tea may also help to keep you and your crew warm.

Waves

Do not bash headlong into large waves. If you must head into the wind, strike them at an angle; however, if at all possible run, on a broad reach with the waves and wind off your windward quarter to avoid broaching, being pooped, or pitch-poling. In more severe conditions, climb overtaking waves at an angle, turn at the crest of the wave, surf down its backside while maintaining an angle of descent that is sufficiently off the wave to slow your speed.

Navigation

Never head for open water in any kind of weather without a GPS, a compass, and charts. Program your GPS for a primary route and an alternate route. If you are running at night, and your GPS goes down or cannot maintain a fix, choose a star or constellation immediately above the horizon and head for it, selecting a new star or constellation as each one sets or rises too far above the horizon to provide a clear target. Cross-check your heading from your chart and GPS and note your heading on your magnetic compass in case your electronics fail.

If you are unable to maintain a GPS fix, figure your distance traveled using dead reckoning (speed x time = distance traveled) and write down your estimate of distance covered every hour. Finally, do not get obsessed on a single destination. Always have a plan and alternate destinations and harbors of refuge if it looks like you will be unable to make your original target without undue risk.

Making decisions

Make your decisions based on *all* the information available at the time. Consider any and all advice from others seriously, but do not allow them to make decisions for you. You are responsible for your boat and the welfare of your crew; although almost all decisions should be discussed and a consensus reached before you take action. If things go bad, remember that most people give up long before their boat.

Above all, remember that fear is your greatest enemy. Do not allow it to cloud your judgment and distract you from staying focused on the task at hand. In this regard, each member of the crew should be given something to do to give them some feeling of control and to moderate the possibility of seasickness.

Finally, deal with each wave and each event one at a time; this is no time for multi-tasking or thinking too far into the future at the cost of dealing with the immediate crisis effectively.

.

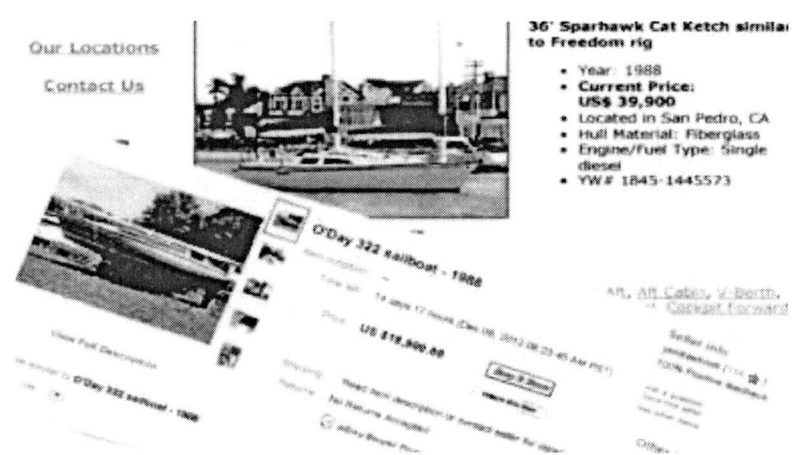

Appendix III
Choosing Just the Right Sailboat

*The sea being smooth
How many shallow bauble boats dare sail
Upon her patient breast.*
  Shakespeare, "Troilus and Cressida"

While Jeanine and I found the right boat for our purposes, you, dear reader, may have entirely different ideas and needs. For those of us who already own a boat that works reasonably well, the standard rule is that we sail what we own, although some changes and improvements, especially in matters of safety and personal comfort, may be important.

Your primary concerns must be affordability, safety, and suitability. Most of us know about people who didn't pay much attention to their cruising requirements and ended up buying the wrong boat. I know of parents with toddlers who bought 16 foot catamarans; novice sailors who were over their heads in high-tech trimarans; large families who stuffed themselves aboard twenty-two foot trailerables (and ended up fighting within minutes after leaving the dock); first time seniors who bought heavy displacement rigs that demanded a truckload of stevedores just to man the winches and raise the sails, and retirees who bought a forty-five footer that required a crew of three to manage. Of course, it's hardly necessary that you make such mistakes yourself. In fact, if you are reasonably prudent, consider all of your options, and make a careful analysis of the pros and cons of each boat you see, you should be able to settle on at least two or three rigs that fit your needs reasonably well and are safe, comfortable, and a pleasure to sail

Boat Design, Accommodations, and Performance.

Although a professional survey of necessary upgrades might be an essential part of the evaluation process, my primary concern here is to discuss how you might find a boat to accommodate your preferences and priorities with regard to accommodations, performance, and safety. Boat designs always involve a compromise. As a rule, speed is achieved at the expense of comfort; weight reduces speed and increases stability; tall, fast boats put the center of pressure high on the sails, which reduces stability and increases heel; adding weight to the keel increases stability but reduces speed; wide-beamed boats have more room below for accommodations, and stability is usually increased, but so is wetted surface and drag--unless the boat has very little draft (excluding the keel), in which case you can expect a good deal of pounding in heavy weather.

If a trailerable is your objective, make sure that your towing vehicle is properly sized to your boat. Most trailerables have a Marconi rig with a retractable keel and rudder, a relatively shallow hull draft, a stayed mast that is typically set amidship, and moderate space below for accommodations. Such boats are adaptable to a variety of weather conditions, and some of them are surprisingly comfortable for small groups who plan to go on extended cruises of one or two weeks.

A terrific number of day sailors, both new and used, are available to individuals who are not especially interested in extended cruises. Pre-owned 12 to 20 foot rigs such as Lasers, Cape Dories, Stars, Hunters, Penguins, O'Days, dories, small catamarans, and the like can be bought for a very modest price, and most of the new, high-tech designs are not particularly expensive. Almost all day sailors are very forgiving and easy to tow and launch, although some do not easily lend themselves to group outings. Without exception, however, they can be beached, which makes them great for camping trips and picnics.

For individuals who are interested in larger exotic or unusual designs, catamarans and trimarans are an interesting option, especially for anyone who likes speed. The larger models are very stable, very fast, and fun to sail. However, most do not run very well to weather, and they can be difficult to tack. In addition, accommodations both above and below tend to be extremely limited unless you choose one of the larger rigs, which can be quite expensive and difficult to moor. On the other hand, the smaller cats and trimarans--though cheaper--are not very well suited for long cruises or families.

Cat boats are stable and wide beamed and have plenty of space below for accommodations; however, since they lack a foresail, they do not beat to weather very well; and they are hard to tack and tend to have a strong weather helm. Also, since they do not have a foresail, they do not have the well-known "slot" between the main and jib; and, hence, they tend to be rather slow.

Ballast, and Stability.

If you are interested in a boat that is superb and steady on a reach and is quite stable, you might consider a shoal keel. As a rule, such boats track very nicely, are typically quite stiff, and rarely pound, even in the roughest conditions. However, they are extremely difficult to back under power--in fact they usually turn in one direction only (a challenge that will compel you to shift quickly between reverse and neutral to 'force' the boat to "coast" and turn in the direction you want to go). Some of the smaller shoal rigs tend to hobby horse in lumpy seas and--like their larger cousins--they do not run very well to weather. If you can get a shoal keel rig to run 45 degrees off the wind, you are indeed lucky but, you are in good company; most cats and catamarans also have trouble sailing to weather. Also, given a large wetted surface, boats with a shoal keel do not have a very sensitive helm; and they usually need a bit of encouragement 140 (backing the jib, for instance) to tack. Sometimes, in light winds, I have found that it is easier to 'chicken jibe' our Mariner ketch--that is, jibe 270 degrees rather than try to drive her through an 80 or 90 degree tack; but then Jeanine and I don't race, we are rarely in a hurry, and we usually single-hand.

Day sailors who are interested in short, overnight trips or simply a day on the water might want to consider one of the many 12-20 foot rigs. Our Victoria 18 pictured here is similar to a Cape Dory, and was a pleasure to sail and very responsive and forgiving. This particular boat was sailed (and trailered) in Florida, the Rocky Mountain High Country, and southern California.

Most trailerable shoal keel rigs can also be difficult to tow and launch because they are typically very heavy (although, given a shallower draft once launched, they can cruise and anchor where rigs with a spade keel cannot go).

Finally, as with any trailerable rig with a non-retractable keel, they rest high on their cradles, which makes them vulnerable to cross winds. In some cases, they may also require a tongue extension or special launching accessories so that they can be backed far enough into the water to float off their cradles.

Most shoal keel rigs are exceptionally stable, and the larger non-trailerable boats almost never pound in rough seas. Our Mariner 31 is comparable in weight to most 36-40 foot boats and will plunge through four foot swells with barely a shiver. In fact, she is inclined to go through the waves rather than over them, and the cockpit can get rather wet as she tosses the waves aside and over the top like just so much confetti. On the other hand, we can anchor much closer to shore because of our shallower draft.

While we are on the subject of keels and stability, it might be worthwhile to discuss water ballast. Although it may increase speed and efficiency on large, high tech racing boats, its primary effect on most trailerables is to ease the strain on the towing vehicle and to make launching easier. However, if you are comfortable about your vehicle's towing capacity, don't especially mind the poorer gas mileage, and feel you have a solid margin of safety on the road, you probably need not be concerned about this option.

Our Balboa 26, *Lady Jeanine*, Boat and trailer weigh approximately 7,000 pounds and are best towed with a 3/4 pickup. Drawing nearly five feet with the keel down, she has can take a sea and has been trailered from Mexico to Canada.

Finally, I would like to put in a word about knock-up, transom mounted rudders. While they are easy to mount and provide considerable latitude for maneuvering in shallows, some of the older models have a tendency to pop to the surface in rough weather. This can make the helm completely unmanageable and usually at the worst imaginable time.

Running Rigging and Sails

It is all too easy to get hung up on the nuances of the latest sail designs (massive roach, carbon fiber materials, etc.); and, unless you plan to do a good deal of racing or feel incorrigibly competitive, most of these innovations will have little relevance.

If you decide on a cruising style trailerable, it is now possible to raise the carbon fiber masts of even some of the largest rigs without a gin pole. This can be a decided advantage if you have to set up your rig alone or if you are a day sailor or a racing enthusiast; however, some of these lighter masts are quite tender and have a low tolerance to strain. Make sure you check the layout, the tolerances, and number of stays on these lighter poles. On the other hand, a good number of the older masts are too heavy to raise alone and will require the use of a gin pole or the assistance of a dock crew. Still, most gin poles are relatively safe; and, if properly set up, they are capable of raising even the heaviest of masts with a minimum of effort.

Regardless of whether you are interested in a trailerable or a larger rig, your running rigging should be relatively simple. A good boat should have a jib and adjustable jib track with block or pulley locks for shortening sail and adjusting the sail shape, depending on whether you want power or speed. Travelers and sheets should be easily accessible from the helm and the main should have at least a Cunningham, outhaul, and vang. On larger rigs, self-tailing winches are a must, and electric winches are always ideal, especially for senior sailors. In most cases, however, they are so expensive as to be prohibitive--in fact, even the prospect of self-tailing winches where needed can kill a sailing budget. In most cases, self-tailing units should be restricted to halyards and jib sheets on boats thirty feet or longer.

Sails.

Minimum requirements for pocket cruisers indicate that you should have a working 6.0 denier main with two sets of reefs and either roller furling or two headsails, a smaller 90 to 110 heavy weather jib and a lighter 160 to 180 sail for light air or down wind runs. You might also want to consider smaller, heavier denier winter sails with very little camber and a jenniker. I hesitate to recommend a spinnaker unless you sail where the winds are constant and predictable. Spinnakers and even jennikers can be deadly where there is a likelihood of a sudden, unexpected gust, storm, or squall, and there are only one or two people to deal with it.

Most seniors will eventually have trouble handling a larger sail plan--indeed, this will eventually result in necessary downsizing. All sailboats require compromises of some sort; large sailboats are safe and comfortable, but usually require a large crew to manage. They are also difficult to maneuver in tight quarters and have a relatively unresponsive helm when a quick turn or stop is required. Their larger sail plan will likely require considerable muscle--although electric winches, though expensive, can minimize the strain for single-handed sailors and seniors.

A larger hull with a smaller sail plan may be ideal in some instances--for example a cutter, a split rig, a ketch, or even a schooner or yawl. Schooners do not run particularly well to windward (hence, they're a rarity), and the sail on a yawl is of little use except when running downwind or tacking. Ketch rigs, like yawls, have a lower CE since their masts are shorter, and they distribute the weight of the sails over two masts instead of one, so the sails are easy to adjust, hoist, and douse. Ketches, schooners, and yawls will have a certain amount of windage because of the extra mast and extra rigging, and on yawls and ketches, the mizzen is practically useless when running to weather (although some ketch sailors have backed the mizzen over the centerline for additional power). On the other hand, two-masted rigs will have a lower center of effort and will heel less, thus assuring a more comfortable ride.

Your sail plan should be set up for a maximum of convenience that will keep you off the deck and in the cockpit as much as possible. You may want to consider installing lazy jacks to avoid climbing topside to secure the main when it is dropped, and roller furling will keep you off the bow (regardless, make sure that your boat has a pulpit so that you will have something to grab if you lose your balance). Roller furling is also invaluable—both as a way of adjusting the size of your headsail from the cockpit and as a quick, safe means of furling without a lot of flogging. A roller furled main is also desirable, but for most seniors on a fixed income, they are so expensive as to be prohibitive.

If you are considering a smaller, trailerable boat, be forewarned that lazy jacks are the devil to set up after launching; and, considering the smaller size of the main, they might be unnecessary. The same might be said of full batten mainsails. While they can ease furling problems and help a full roach sail hold its shape, often as not, they are a needless, added expense on a trailerable or smaller pocket cruiser with a moderate roach.

Regardless of the type of boat you choose, you are may prefer that all halyards be led aft; however, while this will make you less vulnerable to an MOB, they may not always provide much of an advantage–in fact, with trailerables, given the small size of your main and its corresponding light weight, there is a good chance that the sail might jam half way down the track when you try to lower it. On larger rigs, hoisting sail can also be something of a problem unless you are blessed with a titanic winch or electric unit. In my own case, I have found that it is easier and quicker to go up to the mast and hoist our sails while we are inside the breakwater, even though we have a gorilla winch and stopper for just that purpose inside the cockpit. Finally, larger boats with a fractional rig might be easier to handle because of the smaller jib.

The Engine

If you are planning on a trailerable with an outboard, mount the largest engine recommended outboard available. There may be times when you will be faced with extreme tides and heavy winds; and such conditions may tax even the most powerful engine, so do not compromise safety with a small power plant.

While the four cycle outboard units pollute less and offer better mileage, they also take up more space, weigh a good deal more, and are more complicated and therefore more difficult to repair.

Other than the power pack, coil, plugs, and fuel transfer system, there isn't much that can go wrong with a two cycle unit; and they offer a good deal more torque and horse power for the amount of weight involved. Of course, they do not have very good mileage (in the case of a 9.9, the usual auxiliary for a pocket cruiser, they typically burn about a gallon every forty-five minutes at 3/4 throttle), and they are notorious for leaving gallons of unburned gas on pristine cruising grounds.

If your rudder is transom mounted, your engine will have to be mounted to the side, and this may result in some control problems, especially when backing or when you are in a tight moorage. A more desirable option would be to consider a boat whose rudder is located close to the keel. While overall steering is likely to be tender, the outboard can then be transom-mounted directly in line with the keel and rudder, and this will

invariably maximize both control and power. Easily accessible, remote controls for the throttle and gear shift are also desirable for making adjustments with a minimum of effort. They also tend to increase your margin of safety because there is no need to turn away
from the helm to change your speed or shift gears.

Regardless of the size of your boat, inboard gas or diesel engines should be reasonably accessible for servicing and repairs--at least to the degree that you should be able to pump out the old oil, replace it, and replace the filters without going through the agonies of an amateur contortionist. This usually involves removing a number of side panels; but, in any case, good sound insulation is a *must,* especially for boats with a diesel engine, since they can easily generate a below-deck, mind-numbing racket that can destroy the serenity of even the most accomplished monk. Personally, I prefer a diesel auxiliary because they are simple, durable, economical, and forgiving. The newer models do not have to be purged if air gets into the fuel lines--an extraordinary advantage for anyone who has suffered the misfortune of running completely out of fuel and emptying his lines. Diesels are also much safer than gas engines. There is no need to blow out the bilges before starting them, since they are not going to explode and the fumes are not likely to ignite and burn your boat to the waterline. I have heard that if the scientific-experimental types among us light a match and toss it into a pool of diesel, it will go out, although I never had much interest in trying the experiment myself.

Onboard engines do require a bit of extra care. The drive shaft and stuffing box should be checked for leaks; and if the boat is going to be left in storage for any period of time, the fuel tanks should topped to minimize condensation, especially in marine climates. Finally, the engine should be run under load for about a half hour every month or so to get rid of condensation (including water) and any other contaminants.

Diesels also burn less fuel than gas engines. The 65 hp Perkins diesel on our 11,000 pound Mariner 31 burns about 1/2 to 3/4 of a gallon an hour at 6 1/2 knots. The 9.9 four cycle Honda on our 6,000 pound Balboa trailerable burns no less than 3/4 of a gallon in an hour--and it is pushing less than half the weight.

Topside and the Cockpit

Four foot high lifelines, a pulpit and stern pit or stern rail, and jack lines should surround all deck areas aft and forward of the cockpit, and deck surfaces should be coated or taped with non-skid in heavily trafficked areas. Handholds should be easily accessible forward of the cockpit. On larger boats, both the bow and stern should connect to the lifelines to assure adequate handholds at all times.

Our Balboa 26 under sail off Scorpion Bay, Santa Cruz Island in southern California.

On smaller boats, the larger the cockpit, the

smaller the cabin space, so you may want to consider how many people you will take with you for a typical one to three week cruise. If it will usually involve just you and your partner, consider a boat with a larger cabin and smaller cockpit, since the cockpit will hardly be crowded with just the two of you. We have found that our "small" Balboa cockpit barely holds four people, although it can squeeze six if necessary (although, often as not, the ladies sometimes prefer to go below to chat).

In any case, cockpit benches should be relatively comfortable—a plethora of cushions will likely ease some of the back strain, and a bimini can provide some protection from the sun and from splash-over.

Storage space beneath benches should be relatively accessible and should contain emergency PFD's, manual bilge pumps, extra lines and bumpers, and-of course--fuel tanks if the ventilation is good. If not, I would recommend installing extra vents. Cockpit Gauges and controls should be accessible and easy to read from the helm--even from a distance; and, unless you have muscular arms or can steer effectively with your feet, a wheel--not a tiller--is essential on larger rigs that are difficult to balance when on a beat.

Electronics

At the very least, you should have a VHF (we carry an additional handheld unit for emergencies and for use when talking to the harbor police while at the helm). A GPS is also essential--it need not be a fancy unit; a hand-held unit that can be backlit and can be plugged into a receptacle. A depth finder is also important, both for confirming your position with regard to your charts and for locating a secure anchorage that will neither leave you stranded at low tide, caught in the oncoming surf as the tide comes in, or out so deep that you will barely have any scope when setting your anchors. Our radar--though modest--has been invaluable on the Mariner 31, especially since we sail the southern California coast which can be notoriously foggy at times. It also helps us keep track of nearby craft, especially container vessels and commercial traffic. While some mariners also have a special gauge to indicate apparent speed (as opposed to speed over ground), we do not race our boat, so we never saw much need for one, and the GPS is capable of answering any questions about the time of day, ETA (estimated time of arrival), ETE (estimated time enrooted), and the like. A windex will help you to determine the wind direction, since tell-tales are not particularly accurate and change somewhat according to their placement on the sails and on the stays; and a wind speed indicator can be of help in making decisions about when to shorten sail--especially since increases in wind speed can be so subtle that one is hardly aware of the change.

Accommodations

Some boats are filled with so many amenities and are so heavy with every conceivable luxury that they amount to little more than floating campers. I have seen an occasional rig that doesn't even look nautical below deck; which is fine, I guess, for the comfort mavens and those who really don't plan to do much sailing. Usually, however, every extra amenity below deck is going amount to a compromise (or added expense) topside with regard to the stability, sail management, and the sailing aesthetic of the overall boat. Boats with elaborate swim platforms may be easily pooped in a following sea, large windows invite leaks and vulnerability to storms, and excess gadgetry increases expenses and the possibility of a breakdown. On the other hand, an extremely Spartan rig may look like little more than a Purex bottle or--worse yet--an expensive toy.

The below deck layout of a small to mid-size cruiser should be determined by the weather, the number of people you are likely to bring aboard, the time you expect to spend on the water, your love of conveniences, and your age.

Cold, wet climates would indicate a number

of below deck compartments and bulkheads and small hatches and ports in order to keep out the damp and the cold. However, the interiors of such boats can sometimes be rather cave-like and depressing, so you may want to add extra lights, custom sewn curtains and upholstery, and a bevy of colorful pillows and throws. On the other hand, tropical climates would suggest a greater number of hatches and ports and a limited number of bulkheads to keep the interior cool and fresh. Besides, small windows and small ports sometimes give the impression of cruising aboard a U-boat--a not very inviting prospect.

Seniors and retirees will favor a rig with easily accessible hand-holds, moderate entry ladders that do not invite a catastrophic fall; or, preferably, below deck entry stairs so that a person can step comfortably from one level (perhaps a low cabinet) to the next (an engine cover or battery cover or the like). In that regard, entry hatches should be wide and fully removable with plenty of handholds.

A large head with a high toilet is to be preferred--since some of us are a bit arthritic and might have a bit of trouble getting off a toilet that is no higher than a toadstool. The head should be reasonably spacious so that it is possible to turn around without banging into a bulkhead or the door. It should also have easy access sinks that can be used without propping one knee on the head, and you should be able to empty the sink without having to poke around in a dark, lower cabinet in search of a mysterious drain valve.

Individuals who own trailerables with a porta-potti would be well-advised to buy the largest units available. Small units can be something of a pain and embarrassment if they fill up rather quickly; and there is no law that says you can't empty a porta-potti as you pass a pump-out station, even if it is only 1/2 to 3/4 full. Indeed, I have found that this is the preferred option, since a full unit can be rather heavy. I would also strongly recommend a chemical additive to minimize odors.

The head should also have four or five shelves in easy access cabinets--especially in the case of married couples; and onboard heads should be capable of being emptied without having to search through so many valves that even an MIT graduate wouldn't be able to reason his way through the mess.

V-berths should be accessible and not too high above the cabin sole, thick and comfortable with plenty of headroom, and fitted with good lighting for reading, They should have a variety of hatches for good ventilation and long enough so that two people can sleep comfortably without tangling their toes in the bow. Adequate headroom is a must. I have seen some rigs that allow only 3 or 4 feet of headroom in the V-berth, an impossible, cave-like situation when trying to get in or out or when trying to straighten the sheets and blankets in the morning. Most boats, large or small, have a hatch over the V-berth, an important requirement for fresh air buffs and aesthetics who like to sleep under the stars. When inspecting larger rigs with a berth beneath the cockpit, you should walk away if the berth has no exit hatch and is located directly behind the galley, since escape in the event of a galley fire may be impossible.

A well-equipped galley is a must (most seniors love good cookery) with adequate, accessible food storage that requires a minimum of bending and stooping. A well- insulated ice box or even a refrigerator, an inviting dining area, and comfortable seating throughout are also important. A gimbaled propane stove is essential for longer journeys, although our smaller Balboa has a Swedish, non-pressurized alcohol unit that works just fine.

The size of your crew will make a difference in the layout of your accommodations. Seniors who plan to invite their families, including their grandchildren, will probably want a v-berth, quarter berths, convertible port and starboard benches, plenty of storage areas, and, of course, an enclosed head with a sink. Smaller boats will likely eliminate any concern about a large dining table or galley. Such "luxuries" will invariably expand your cabin and compromise the size of your cockpit. On the other hand, you shouldn't have to feel that your accommodations must look like the inside of a Purex bottle. They can be enhanced quite nicely with finished wooden floorboards, bulkheads, and panels; shaded, incandescent lights; and bright, custom-sewn upholstery and lots and lots of cushions; and a cd player, good reading lights, and a library of good books.

Ground Tackle and the Tender

You may also want to check the ground tackle on any prospect you are considering. Most mid-size cruisers should have at least two anchors— perhaps a Danforth and a plow or CQR—on ten or fifteen feet of chain and 4
about 200-400 feet of rode. This, however, is the bare minimum; I would suggest at least two other anchors and an equal amount of rode. Check with your local chandlery for the appropriate sizes and weights. We usually go one size larger than necessary just for peace of mind.

If you are planning on a trailerable without an anchor winch, be wary of the heavier anchors such as a CQR (usually a plow will do just about the same job), since you are probably going to have to haul these monsters from the deeps without the help of a winch. Of course, power winches are an absolute necessity for larger rigs. Some of the older, larger rigs have manual anchor winches, but they are extremely slow and cumbersome.

Finally, you will probably need a tender. An inflatable is the preferred option. They weigh less and tow with a minimum of effort. They can also serve as a life raft, since they are not likely to sink and are relatively stable and therefore not as likely to capsize. I have found that, for the small investment involved and in the interest of safety, it is a good idea to buy a small outboard for puttering about and exploring hidden coves and sandy beaches.

Conclusion

Of course, nothing can replace the expertise of a qualified surveyor or good broker. Even so, while they will search out the condition of a boat and make a recommendation regarding problems of wear and replacement costs, they may not be able to be entirely helpful in providing certain kinds of advice about the kind of rig that best suits your personal preferences and meets your individual needs. That is something that you probably know best; and, if you consider the pros and cons involved in evaluating performance, accommodations, sail plan, rigging, power plant, and electronics, then perhaps you will be in a better position to decide whether a particular rig is just the right boat for you.

Lady Jeanine being prepared for launching in Seattle and a tour north to Canada. The 4x4 in the foreground is a gin pole which provides leverage to raise the mast.

Once you have made your decision, you might want to call on a qualified surveyor to make certain that the boat is safe, well found, and indicates no abnormal amount of wear or corrosion.

On the other hand, if the systems are relatively

simple and the boat is under twenty-six feet, this may not be necessary.

Sidebar:
Buying a Boat: Making it Easier

Research the boats that interest you: *Use the internet boat webs to get some idea of what kind of boat you want (including photos of the interior layout) and to get an idea of price and availability. Check the manufacturer's web page and the local library for information about performance, stability (See Appendix V), customer loyalty and enthusiasm, and durability.*
Be prepared to compromise: *Approach boat-buying with a certain amount of suspicion, much as you would if you were buying a car or purchasing a home--and remember, you're probably not going to get everything you want,*

either because you will be priced out of the market or because you will be looking at too small or too large a rig to suit your cruising style. Also, passage-makers, live-a-boards, and racers should be regarded with a certain amount of suspicion, since they have typically been stressed or not sailed at all. In either case, the boat will probably require an extensive refit.

Match your prospects to suit your abilities and cruising style: *In most cases, as seniors, comfort, ease of handling, and stability will probably be more important than speed. Most important, don't consider a boat that will can't be single-handed-or, at the very least, managed by you and your partner. Big boats (with all their wonderful amenities) require big crews, so choose a sail plan that will be relatively easy to manage.*

First things first: *If you plan to buy a pre-owned boat, concentrate on essentials: the hull (any leaks?), standing rigging, engine, and thru-hulls; and the condition of the deck (watch for delamination and leaks), chain plates, electrical systems, keel bolts, and blistering.*

You will probably have to move your boat shortly after you close the sale: *In most cases, you should expect to lose your slip shortly after you close your sail. Be prepared for the trials and tribulations of moving the boat and* finding a new moorage (See Chapter III and IV).

Be prepared for extra expenses: Set aside extra money for updates and refits--just as you would if you bought a used car or pre-owned home. Even a new boat may require a certain number of additional expenses such as a dingy and dingy motor, extra electronics, self-steering, a bimini or dodger, interior customized amenities, and the like.

Be Prepared for complications when closing: In some states, for example, Colorado, buying a boat is no different from buying a washer and dryer. In others, it is very complicated. In California, for instance, licensing is handled by the DVM, liens must be cleared, and the title and exchange of funds must be verified. Hence, it may not be possible to close a sale for a number of days.

Appendix IV

Calculating Boat and Sail Performance

*Now is the season of sailing;
for already the chattering swallow is come and the pleasant west wind; ....*
             Leonidas of Tarentum, 274 B.C.

Calculating boat and sail dimensions and performance can be a pretty complicated affair-- perhaps even a bit exotic. Some of the calculations are important to race committees when handicapping different rigs; others are of value if you're concerned about stability or manageability. For instance, the D/L or displacement/length ratio is a good way to determine a boat's weight for her size, especially in comparison with other boats. A boat with a light displacement for her length is going to be fast, difficult to steer and sail, and relatively unstable--especially in dirty weather. As a rule, a boat with a D/L ratio of 325 or over is a heavy rig, 200-325 is light to moderate, anything less than 200 is a very light displacement racer. Anything less than 125 is an ultra-light and falls into the ULDB category. Unless you're a speed demon, you will probably want to stay away from these lighter rigs. Finally, length overall (LOA.) refers to a boat's length from the tip of the bow to the back of the stern; the waterline length (LWL) is the forward-most and aft-most points of the hull along the waterline. Older boats had a much longer LOA than LWL or overhang at the bow and stern. As a consequence, the LWL increased exponentially as the boat heeled. This increased the boat's maximum hull speed and allowed it to go faster. More recent designs have moderated the differences between the LOA and the LWL, so these figures are not as significant in figuring a boat's handicap if you plan to do any racing.

The sail area to displacement ratio (SA/D) compares the weight of the boat with the amount of sail area. In some ways, it is a rather limited calculation, since it assumes that weight is the only limitation on speed and performance. Most fast cruising rigs have a SA/D ratio of 14-16; motor sailors and heavy water rigs have ratios of 8-13.

The center of effort or CE is the center or balance point for all the aerodynamic forces that play on the sail. The center of lateral resistance or CLR refers to the underbody or that part of the hull which is underwater. It should be just aft of the CE. to assure a minimum 3 degree weather helm-- which assures that the boat will swing into the wind if the helm is released. On some cats and experimental rigs, the CE is forward of the CLR, which can make them extremely dangerous in a high wind, because rather than swing into the wind and right themselves, they will swing off the wind, increasing the likelihood of a capsize.

The capsize ratio provides a means of determining at what point a boat will capsize and not right itself. It is determined by the Capsize Screening Formula or CSF. As a rule, a capsize ratio of 2.0 or less is desirable; anything more would suggest a somewhat tender rig. The range of positive stability is the point at which a boat will heel and not right itself. A dingy, for example, might have an RPS of about 80 degrees; whereas an ocean rig will heel as much as 120 degrees and still right itself.

Most boat owners are also likely to be concerned about the Ballast/Displacement ratio. This refers to the amount of ballast in a boat's keel as it relates to a boat's overall weight. A stiff boat will probably have ratio of about 40 degrees of more, whereas a racer might average below 30 degrees.

Finally, most sailboat owners will be

concerned about hull speed--the theoretical maximum speed of a boat's hull. It is essentially determined by a boat's length and the point at which the hull is located precisely in the middle of the trough between the bow and stern. Any attempt to go faster would force the boat to "climb" out of the trough to get over the first wave, essentially canceling the positive effect of loading on more sail or increasing the throttle. However, some boats such as our Balboa 26 trailerable are quite capable of surfing through rough waters in a high wind and can thus go much faster than their theoretical hull speed. And, of course, catamarans and trimarans pose a whole new set of problems and mathematical variables.

None of these calculations can truly explain the complete picture; and, among boat designers, there are so many variables that the art of increasing boat speed and sailing efficiency is probably the exclusive territory of wizards, a select genius or two, and a committee of extra-terrestrials. This is because boat and sail design involve a complex mix of physics, hydrology, wind pressures, and innumerable other variables. For example, one might consider the effects of a bulb keel, a shallow draft rig, spade keels, shoal keels, dual keels, carbon fiber sails, sails with a tremendous amount of roach, schooners, ketches, cats, the size and rake of the rudder and keel, and very likely a thousand other considerations. In fact, I have a 300+ page book in my library dedicated exclusively to sail design and sail performance--and nothing more.

Finally, all of the calculations and ratios discussed here have specific mathematical formulas which can be applied to a specific rig. I won't burden you with them here, but if your curiosity gets the better of you, you can find them in the <u>Annapolis Book of Seamanship</u> and on the web.

In choosing or evaluating the performance of a boat that interest you, it is important to consider some of the more important data described above. Such data can sometimes be acquired by consulting the manufacturer's specs, researching the web, or reading the information offered on a specific chat group or owner's web. You may also want to check out a candidate's data or the data on your present boat to make sure it is designed for the kind of cruising you have in mind.

For instance, Jeanine and I are not particularly interested in speed, but we do favor a classic rig that is stable and easy to manage. We chose a Mariner 31 ketch because, while not very fast, she is very stiff with a capsize ratio of 1.71--far below the ratio for an ocean rig; her range of positive stability is 120 degrees, and you can't get much better than that; her SA/D is 13.97 which qualifies her as capable of taking a sea; her ballast to displacement ratio is 43%, far above the average of 35%, and her maximum hull speed is 6.8 knots, although I doubt that she would ever even come close, since her SA/D is 13.97. However, Jeanine and I are in no hurry to get anywhere once we board her; and we *do* enjoy a stable, comfortable rig that can take a sea.

Appendix V

Scandia Dream's Checklist

------Getting Under Way
1. At all times: Propane: tank and stove–Closed
2. Set out tethers, harnesses, pfd's
3. Shore power–disconnect & stow
4. Anchors–rode coiled, anchors secured
5. Seacocks-close head & sink
6. Bidata, gps, vhf – ON
7. Unhook ladder if at anchor; set painters close to transom and secure
8. Open raw water to engine, minimum throttle, neutral gear
9. *Start Motor* and check raw water exhaust for good flow/steam; check amps, oil, engine temp
10. Bow and stern lines: coiled on deck while pulling out
11. After pulling out-- stow bumpers

---at ports of call---------------------–
1. Tie dingy to side of boat
2. Set out ladder, hook safety lanyard

---Returning home:
1. Set out bumpers, mooring lines at breakwater
    Then, at dock
2. Raw water seacock closed
3. Connect shore power–if leaving boat, 12v Off; seacocks (galley, head) closed
4. VHF, bidata, radar-Off, propane tank: Off
5. Secure dingy, lock motor in cockpit, store dingy fuel tank beneath bench with utility tanks
6. Pack and check drawers, galley, counter tops, microwave, cupboards
7. Lock ports
8. Pack cameras, film, wallet, checkbook, address book, ship's log
9. Double check all mooring lines, bumpers
10. "Heat" light (110v) **ON**; battery charger **ON-- set timer: 1/2 hour daily**
11. Double lock boat

Appendix VI

Suggested Reading

(where no publisher is noted, the book is available from a number of different publishers).

A cruising guide and adequate charts and tide tables for your particular venues! See also "References and Suggested Additional Reading," Chapter X, "First Aid and Safety

---

Brewer. Ted. <u>Ted Brewer Explains Sailboat Design.</u> Camden, ME: International Marine, 1987.

Brown, Larry. <u>Sailing on a Microbudget.</u> Camden, ME, International Marine, 1984 (small cruising boats).

Calder, Nigel. <u>Marine Diesel Engines: Maintenance, Troubleshooting, and Repair.</u> Camden, ME: International Marine, 1987 (first-rate engine manual).

Chapman Piloting: Seamanship & Small Boat Handling. 62nd ed. New York: Hearst Marine Books, 1996 (this book should be the foundation and ready reference of any ship's library).

Coles, K. Allard. Heavy Weather Sailing. Camden, ME: International Marina, 1992 (a classic).

Collins, Mike. Fitting Out a Fibreglass Hull. Dobbs Ferry, NY: Sheridan House, 1990.

Compton, Peter. Troubleshooting Marine Diesels. Camden, ME: International Marine, nd (this book has saved me on a number of occasions).

Conrad, Joseph. The Nigger of the Narcissus & also Lord Jim (two of the best by one of the best writers of the sea-compelling; they belong in every ship's library).

Coote, Jack. Total Loss. Dobbs Ferry, NY: Sheridan House, 1985 (a classic).

Dana, Richard Henry. Two Years Before the Mast. (belongs in every ship's library--a compelling read).

Djos, Matts. The Sacrament of Sail: Finding Our Way. Amazon.com, 2011 (a narrative of sailing adventures and misadventures in California, the Pacific Northwest, Canada, and the Southwest).

- - -. Cruising the West: Fifty Years of Sail. Amazon.com, 2012 (revised version of The Sacrament of Sail. Includes an additional chapter on Mexico).

- - -. The Spindrift: a Love Story. Amazon.com, 2012 (a novel, includes numerous sailing scenes).

Duffet, John. Boat Owners' Guide to Modern Maintenance. New York: Norton, 1985 (essential tools and skills for boat maintenance).

Dunlap, G.D. and H.H. Shufeldt. Dutton's Navigation & Piloting. 14th ed. Annapolis, MD: Naval Institute Press, 1985 (a classic--very thorough).

Hemingway, Ernest. The Old Man and the Sea. New York: Scribner's, 1952 (of course!).

Henderson, Richard. *Understanding Rigs and Rigging*. Camden, ME: International Marine, 1990.

Herreshoff, Halsey C., Ed. The Sailor's Handbook. Boston: Little, Brown and Company, 1983 (a classic).

Hinz, Earl. The Complete Book of Anchoring and Mooring. Centreville, MD: Cornell Maritime, 1986.

Homer. The Odyssey (the first great sea story)

Howard, Jim. Handbook of Offshore Cruising: The Dream and Reality of Modern Ocean Cruising. Dobbs Ferry, NY: Sheridan House, 1994.

Kenney, Dick. Looking at Sails. Camden, ME: International Marine, 1988.

Kotch, William J. Weather for the Mariner. 3rd edition. Annapolis: Naval Institute Press, 1983.

Larkin, Frank J. Basic Coastal Navigation: An Introduction to Piloting. Dobbs Ferry, NY: heridan House, 1995 (a complex subject made simple and manageable).

London, Jack. The Voyage of the Snark (a minor classic).

Melville, Herman. Moby Dick (a must!).

Nichols, Peter. Sea Change: Alone Across the Atlantic in a Wooden Boat. New York: Viking, 1997 (truly an enjoyable, compelling read with curiously informative digressions).

- - -. A Voyage for Madmen. New York: Perennial, Harper Collins, 2002.

Nicolson, Ian. Surveying Small Craft. 3rd edition. Dobbs Ferry, NY: Sheridan House, 1994 (a classic).

Norgrove, Ross. Cruising Rigs and Rigging. Camden, ME: International Marine, 1982.

Pardey, Lin and Larry. The Capable Cruiser. New York: W.W. Norton, 1987 (a guide to long-distance cruising).

Roberts, John, and Maria Mann. Choosing Your Boat. New York: Norton, 1986.

Ross, Wallace. Sail Power. New York: Knopf, 1975 (very technical but thorough).

Rusmaniere, John. The Annapolis Book of Seamanship, illus Mark Smith. New York: Simon & Schuster, 1989. (Next to Chapman, this is the second most important book and ready-reference in your   ship's library).

- - -, The Sailing Lifestyle. New York: Simon & Schuster, 1985 (basic sailing and cruising skills).

Slocum, Miles. Sailing Alone Around the World, 1900 (a classic among classics. The first single-handed circumnavigation. This book belongs in every ship's library).

Spurr, Daniel. <u>Upgrading the Cruising Sailboat.</u> Camden, ME: Seven Seas, 1990.

Van Doren, W.G. <u>Oceanography and Seamanship.</u> Centreville, MD: Cornell Maritime Press, 1992.

Verne, Michael. <u>The Complete Bok of Yacht Care.</u> 2nd ed. Dobbs Ferry: Sheridan House, 1993.

Index

Accommodations & amenities, 31-32, 34, 43-44, 146-48, 149-54
Advantages of maturity, 21-22, 109-118
Advice for beginners, 119-128
Anchoring, 128, 158
Ballast and stability, 139-40
Baja Peninsula, 11-12
Balboa 26 (*Lady Jeanine*), 11-21
Big Sur, 98-99
Brokers, 33-34, 35
Closing a sale, 41-42
Common sense sailing, maturity, 21-25
Dana, Richard Henry, 6
Djos, Matts &Jeanine, v-vi
Durability (seniors) 74-75
Electronics, 152-54
Engines, 32, 37-39, 147-50
Expenses of a refit, 53-55, 56
Fatigue, 73-75
Fear, 18
Forgetfulness, 85-86
Ground tackle and tender, 158-59
Heavy weather sailing, 129-34

  Engine management, 130-31
  Navigation, 133-34
  Safety, 131-32
  Sail management, 130
  Waves, 133
Holmes, Oliver Wendell, 27
Hypothermia, 81-82
Injuries (onboard), 84-85
Inspections, 35-37
  Essentials, 35-37, 41, 130-31, 158
  Procedure, 35-40
Internet surveys, 29-30, 33
Long Beach & San Pedro (CA), 107-8
Manufacturer's/owner's web pages, 29-30
Monterey (CA) 95, 97, 98-99
MOB (man overboard) 84-85
Moderation, 24-25
Moorages and marinas
  Access (channels), 66-70
  Amenities, 62-63. 65-66
  Pollution 64-65
  Rates, 59-63
  Requirements, 59, 61, 65-66, 123-26, 128
  Security, 60-61
Morrow Bay (CA), 100-01
Moss Landing (CA), 96-97
Navigation, 7-8, 17-18

Penn, William, 73
Point Conception and Point Arguello, 101-3
Prescriptions and medical supplies, 75-76
Pricing a boat, 40-48. 138, 160-61
Publius Syrus Maximus, 129
Refits--setting priorities, 47-50
Rossetti, Dante Gabriel, 5
Safety, 59, 61, 65-66, 1234-6, 128
Sail plans, 33, 144-147
San Carlos (MX), 11-12, 19-20
San Simeon, 99
Santa Barbara (CA), 104-5
Santa Catalina Island (CA), 106-7
Seasickness, 77-78
Sea of Cortez (MX), 11-21, 23-24
Security
    Moorages, 60
    Onboard, 90-91
Skin care, 78-80
Sun stroke, heat exhaustion, 77-78
Stability (formulas for sailboats), 120, 121-2, 165-70
Surveys, 39
Trailerable boats, 140-42, 155-56
Tennyson, Alfred Lord, 11
U;lysses, 11, 25
Wolcott, Derek, 95

plan 16 57 5⁹⁵